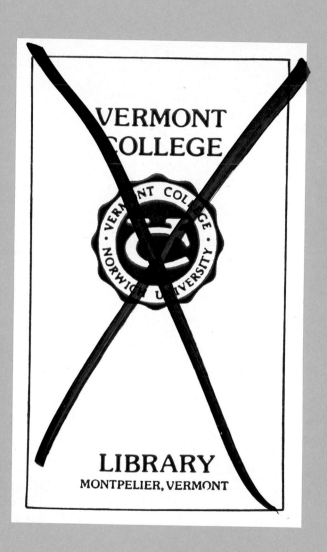

Stress and Policing

Stress and Policing

Sources and Strategies

Jennifer M. Brown
Research Department, Hampshire Constabulary, UK

and

Elizabeth A. Campbell
Department of Psychology, University of Surrey, UK

JOHN WILEY & SONS

Chichester · New York · Brisbane · Toronto · Singapore

Other Wiley Editorial Offices

John Wiley & Sons, Inc., 605 Third Avenue,
New York, NY 10158-0012, USA

Jacaranda Wiley Ltd, 33 Park Road, Milton,
Queensland 4064, Australia

John Wiley & Sons (Canada) Ltd, 22 Worcester Road,
Rexdale, Ontario M9W 1L1, Canada

John Wiley & Sons (SEA) Pte Ltd, 37 Jalan Pemimpin #05-04,
Block B, Union Industrial Building, Singapore 2057

Library of Congress Cataloging-in-Publication Data

Brown, Jennifer M.
    Stress and policing : sources and strategies / Jennifer M. Brown
    and Elizabeth A. Campbell
        p.   cm.
    Includes bibliographical references and index.
    ISBN 0-471-94138-7 (cased)
    1. Police—Job stress.   2. Police—Great Britain—Job Stress.
    I. Title.
    HV7936.J63B78   1994
    363.2'2'019—dc20   93-28406
                                                          CIP

British Library Cataloguing in Publication Data

A catalogue record for this book is available from the British Library

ISBN 0-471-94138-7 (cased)

Typeset in 11/13pt Palatino from author's disks by Text Processing Department,
John Wiley & Sons Ltd, Chichester
Printed and bound in Great Britain by Biddles Ltd, Guildford, Surrey

To A.M.C.

Contents

Contents

CHAPTER 1

Introduction

The aims of this book are to examine critically beliefs about the nature of stress experienced by police officers; to clarify the state of knowledge and research in this area; and to identify means of dealing with the adverse consequences of exposure to stressors.

It has long been recognised that police officers may be involved in a range of traumatic situations because of the nature of their duties. However it is only relatively recently that the concept of Post Traumatic Stress Disorder has become widely used to describe the adverse somatic, behavioural and emotional sequelae of extremely stressful events such as shooting incidents, major public disorders, multiple car accidents as well as other large-scale disasters. The question of whether the more routine or everyday stressors that police officers are exposed to can lead to adverse effects on the individual has also now begun to be addressed. The text will address in turn the sources of stress in police work, the consequences arising from that stress and ways of dealing with both the sources and consequences.

STRESS IN THE WORKFORCE

Research investigations into the effects of occupational stress began in the 1950s (cf Beehr and O'Hara 1987). It is now accepted and well documented that high levels of stress among employees, whether induced at work or by personal problems, can reduce productivity. This has become an issue of increased interest in both the public and private sectors in recent years. The costs to employers of stress-related illness, which can contribute to absen-teeism, high employee turnover, early retirement on health grounds and premature death, are considerable and increasing.

Governmental studies in the United States have estimated that billions of dollars are lost in industrial productivity losses because of stress-related illnesses (Beehr and O'Hara 1987). In the United Kingdom, attitudes to the problem of stress have been changing as the benefits of employee health and welfare are increasingly recognised. Concern about the adverse consequences of stress is growing amongst all sectors of the working population. Employ-ers are increasingly introducing employee welfare programmes and counselling schemes, such as the employee advisory resource programme recently piloted by the British Post Office (Allison, Cooper and Reynolds 1989). However, such initiatives are still the exception, and despite a clear increase in and awareness of stress as a problem generally, a recent Health Education report found that employers' responses to stress were at best piecemeal if they existed at all (Health Education Authority 1988).

STRESS IN THE POLICE SERVICE

A number of factors have contributed to the considerable growth of interest in the causes and effects of stress among police officers. For example, in Britain in the early 1980s a working party was commissioned by the Association of Chief Police Officers and the Home Office to study the effects of occupational stress

on the health, well-being and work performance of police officers. The outcome of this study was a report *Stress in the Police Service* (Association of Chief Police Officers 1984). Since that time a number of British police forces have responded to the recommen-dations contained in the report, and have set up local schemes to promote health and welfare and to offer counselling services.

Chief Police Officers have pragmatic as well as welfare concerns about the availability of police personnel. This concern has been fuelled by increasing pressures on public services in general to be economically rational (eg Home Office 1983); by increasing demands being made on the resources of the police service in particular (Hayes 1988); and also by the impact of the problems of absenteeism and early retirement, and their exacerbating effect on personnel shortages (House of Commons Home Affairs Committee 1991).

Also in Britain a series of disasters (the Bradford City football stadium fire and the Manchester Airport fire in 1985, the sinking of the Zeebrugge ferry in 1987 and latterly the deaths of football supporters in the Hillsborough stadium disaster) stimulated interest in disaster preparedness, prevention and management in general, and an increasing awareness of the stress experienced by police officers and other professional helpers involved in disaster work. This interest stimulated further concern about other potential sources of stress which were recognised as deriving from the police service's own management style and organisational systems. Thus from one extreme, where officers were expected to absorb the vicissitudes of their job without any organisational support, it is now felt by some critics that stress has become so institutionalised that recourse to counselling becomes an excuse to mitigate the consequences of poor performance. It is important therefore to assess the status of the concept of stress as it applies to the police service before offering remedial prescriptions.

CRITICAL ISSUES

Certainly within the media, and to some extent amongst police and academic sources, the basic assumptions that police work is stressful and that police officers suffer from stress at a greater rate than other occupational groups tend to have been accepted rather uncritically. Cooper, Davidson and Robinson (1982) reviewed American research which indicated concern over the apparently higher incidence of stress-related illness and suicide rates amongst police officers compared with other occupations. Malloy and Mays (1984), however, query the assumptions in such studies of stress in the police by asking the following questions :

(i)   What are the sources of police stress?
(ii) Are they unique to law enforcement?

(iii)   Does the literature provide empirical support showing that law enforcement is inherently more stressful than other occupations?

(iv)   Is there a demonstrable relationship between police stress and psychological, physical and social dysfunction?

These authors conclude that the hypothesis that police are amongst the most stressed occupational groups has little consistent empirical support. Threats of physical harm and participation in violence are often cited as potential stressors unique to the police (Kroes 1982). Not only do other groups, particularly emergency services personnel and professional carers, face violence, but as Malloy and Mays (1984) point out:

> presently it is difficult to say how much stress is associated with law enforcement or to define the direct consequences of this stress. Whilst most writers have assumed a priori that police work precipitates high stress levels there has been a growing awareness that many past assumptions may not be valid.

Webb and Smith (1980) find that the evidence is "contradictory" in terms of whether or not police work is more stressful than other occupations, but suggest that this is actually a "specious" issue. More important is the need to identify sources of stress and their consequences together with devising procedures to prevent or alleviate these.

A second set of issues relate to the definition of stress and the operationalisation of the concept. In a review of these difficulties, Marmot and Madge (1987) indicate that there is not only disagreement about the meaning of the term and how to measure it, but also a lack of understanding about the causal route from the experience of stress to being ill. They suggest that it might be helpful to differentiate between stressors, perceived stress and ascribed stress.

Stressors generally mean some environmental circumstances which may directly or indirectly affect an individual. Perceived stress relates to that which is subjectively experienced by an individual, whilst ascribed stress is some external and more objective assessment of adverse consequences suffered by a person. A full discussion of these problems of describing and assessing stress is given in Brown and Harris (1978) and in Kasl and Cooper (1987).

The nature and status of the available evidence pertaining to police stress need to be noted. For example in some areas such as stress among senior women officers or homosexual officers, there is little systematic research and most of the evidence comes from personal accounts. These accounts are of value in that they indicate areas of concern but clearly caution must be exercised in generalising from these descriptions to the population of police officers. Other evidence is more robust in that it stems from research efforts employing sound research design and methodology. Another class of evidence is that deriving from the evaluation literature where the effectiveness of some intervention is being assessed. Beehr and O'Hara (1987) have described the varieties of and explanatory power of evaluative studies. Such studies range from the uninterpretable to strong designs in which all the necessary methodological requirements are in place.

Finally, stress research is beset by difficulties of establishing pathways linking particular stressors to physical and/or psychological reactions. There is usually no simple dose relationship, ie the risk of adverse consequences does not increase as a linear function of increased exposure. Some personal or social characteristics may both predispose an individual's exposure and at the same time also mitigate or exacerbate adverse consequences. Marmot and Madge (1987) advise on the importance of elaborating and testing an explicit model which specifies clearly the definitions of the terms used and the nature of the links between various factors when gathering and analysing data in this area.

SOME FACTORS UNDERLYING POLICE FORCES' INTEREST IN STRESS

There remains the possibility that some aspects of the "police stress" issue might be socially constructed for certain political purposes rather than reflecting true concerns for health and welfare. There is therefore a need to identify factors which might colour the views adopted by those who either promote or minimise

the idea of stress as a problem for the police. Such factors might
include:

- *Malingerers' charter.* Individuals in the police service who
  may use stress as the psychological equivalent of a "bad
  back" in order to claim or exaggerate occupationally related
  ill-health.
- *Vested interest.* Making stress an issue could be a vehicle for
  vested interests. For example, bureaucratic initiatives may
  be driven by wider political considerations; police staff
  associations might be thought to be inflating the issue in
  order to increase their bargaining powers; senior officers
  may be looking for ways to appear innovative or to show
  concern for the interests of their staff.
- *Stress bandwagon.* External stress consultants and in-house
  advisers will want to encourage the flow of resources. Police
  managers might feel pressure to keep up to date with the
  fashionable topic of stress and to be seen to be promoting
  remedial measures.

It is important to acknowledge the presence of such views and
their potential influence when identifying the causes, effects and
treatment of stress-related problems.

ASSUMPTIONS AND QUESTIONS IN POLICE STRESS

There are, then, a number of assumptions about the nature of
police stress which can be discerned in the police stress literature.
These are summarised in Table 1. A careful review of the literature
reveals that much evidence supporting these assumptions stems
from personal opinions based on anecdote, or from the results of
police force in-house group discussions and the reports of Working Parties from individual police forces. The available empirical
evidence is often methodologically limited or contradictory. Further, claims made usually confuse a number of issues which
should more rightly be kept distinct. Any approach to the problem
of stress within the police service should consider the following
separate issues:

- *Understanding the problem.* The questions involved must be teased apart in order to identify the extent of the problem and the key issues involved.
- *Discovering cause and effect.* To do this it is necessary to collect and evaluate empirical evidence.
- *Implementing solutions.* A full understanding of the issues involved and of the causes and effects of stress will make it possible to decide what mix of primary (preventive), secondary (removal of adverse conditions) and tertiary (damage limitation) remedial measures should be taken in order to tackle the problem.

The assumptions found in the police stress literature which have been summarised in Table 1 will be reviewed below.

Table 1.   Assumptions about the nature of police stress

1.   Police work is inherently stressful

2.   Police officers suffer the negative effects of stress to a significant degree

3.   Police work is more stressful than other types of work

4.   The police deserve special attention to reduce causes and consequences of stress

5.   Police work will become even more stressful in the future

Source: adapted from Malloy and Mays (1984). The police stress hypothesis: A critical evaluation. *Criminal Justice and Behaviour*, **II**, 197–224.

Police Work is Inherently Stressful and Police Officers Suffer the Negative Effects of Stress to a Significant Degree

Stress is a fact of life and there is no reason to suppose that police officers are any more immune from the wear and tear imposed by life events or working environments than other workers. Nevertheless, to establish any claim that the police are particularly under stress it must be shown both that (i) police work is inherently stressful and that (ii) police officers suffer from the effects of exposure to work-related stressors. These are two distinct conditions which must be validated with different kinds of information. In the absence of convincing empirical studies which link high levels of stress to aspects of police work, it cannot be said that these conditions have been met.

Even if it can be established that policing is a potentially stressful job, this does not necessarily imply that police officers will suffer psychological distress. There is a dominant police ideology which maintains that officers should be emotionally strong individuals able to handle incidents and situations which would prove stressful to civilians. It is therefore necessary for any discussions or recommendations to distinguish clearly between measures of potential stressors to which the police are exposed and measures of any symptoms of distress actually occurring in the officers.

If the level of police stress is no greater than that experienced by the working population in general, it could be argued that no special action need be taken on the part of the police. Police officers could simply avail themselves of the various stress management techniques and treatments available.

However, even if systematically conducted research were to show that police stress is not experienced at a critical level—ie insufficient to affect the efficiency or cost-effectiveness of the service—there might still be a need for action on welfare grounds. As well as this, welfare interventions could be effective in creating a more positive working environment in which to obtain a high level of commitment and productivity from the workforce, purely in terms of organisational self-interest.

Police Work is More Stressful than other Types of Work

It has been argued that the police are subject to more stress than other workers because of the special nature of their job: for example, they witness death and mutilation, deal with violent criminals, and are involved in potentially life-threatening situations (Territo and Vetter 1981). Alternatively it can be argued that these "traumatic events" are rare and that officers simply suffer from higher levels of the same kind of routine stressors experienced by other workers.

It is important to keep these elements (their causes and the effects) separate because they have different policy implications. It is not sufficient merely to establish that police officers are highly stressed, policy-makers also need to know what factors are responsible for such stress in order to justify the time and expense of undertaking appropriate remedial measures.

If police officers experience more stress or distress because of factors unique to their work, there may be no way to remove the potential stressors short of society changing the demands made on its police officers. The job may simply entail unavoidable stressors. If the causes of stress cannot be eliminated, ways must be found to alleviate them or treat the symptoms, and this may involve developing programmes specifically designed for the police.

However, if police officers are subject to high levels of occupational stressors which are not unique to police work, there may be no need to develop police-specific programmes. Rather, stress management programmes developed by other sectors could be adopted by the police, and the organisation and management of police work reviewed so as to reduce these sources of occupational stress. In this case, the problem is identified as internal to the organisation rather than external, and it should be possible to eliminate many of the negative sources of stress, given enough resources and management commitment.

The Police Deserve Special Action to Reduce Causes and Consequences of Stress

Many senior police managers and rank and file service members still believe that stress is not a problem requiring priority attention. Such beliefs are based on one of three lines of reasoning:

(i)   Police officers do not show serious symptoms of stress because whatever the demands of the job, they are able to cope psychologically and not suffer adverse consequences. This has been termed the "John Wayne Syndrome" (Gresty and McLelland 1989), and essentially involves denying that stress is a significant problem.

(ii)   Stress exists but there is nothing to be done because the problem is in the very nature of the job which cannot be changed. By denying that anything can be done, this view precludes questions of whether anything should be done.

(iii)   Some action to alleviate the causes and effects of stress should ideally be taken. But limited resources and social policy considerations make this a low priority. Proponents of this line of reasoning acknowledge that stress is a problem, and are therefore open to arguments that some action should be taken for reasons of organisational self-interest or on humanitarian grounds. Attempts have been made to define a threshold of reduced efficiency due to stress, below which remedial action is acknowledged to become cost-effective. However, quantitative information on the reduction of efficiency due to stress, its financial cost and the likely effectiveness and cost of remedial action has rarely been available.

The accumulation of evidence, however, does indicate that stress levels within the police do play a significant role in absenteeism and wastage through early retirement. The levels are such as to make the above views less tenable in the light of good human resource management.

It is often stated that it takes a particular type of person to be a police officer, or that the service attracts, or at least retains, people with rather specific characteristics. A variety of studies, mostly from the USA, have suggested that police officers are more likely to have personalities that are "authoritarian", "conservative", "dogmatic", "cynical", "loyal" or "prejudiced". Findings from these studies are inconclusive, and none distinguishes clearly whether this is due more to personality factors and/or social background than to occupational socialisation within the job. Significantly less work has been undertaken on British police officers and care must be exercised in extrapolating findings from one culture to another (Davidson and Veno 1980).

The existence of a particular "police personality" is potentially significant, because of individual differences in response to stressors (White 1982). If it could be demonstrated that certain personality types were better suited to police work than others, then stress problems could be attributed to the recruitment of stress-prone individuals. There is even the possibility that any high levels of psychological distress observed amongst police officers may have arisen because they were more susceptible to the effects of stress rather than subject to higher levels of routine stressors or to particularly stressful factors peculiar to the police service. There is also the question of whether the need to live up to police ideologies is stressful in itself (White 1982).

There are some who argue that the police deserve special help in reducing both the causes and the consequences of stress regardless of whether they are more stressed than other sectors of the working population because of the special role played by the police service in society. Manolias (1983) puts forward the following reasons why stress in the police service should be given special consideration by the police and the public alike:

(i)   The police, among others, fulfil an essential function in society. This requires an effective workforce and stress potentially undermines the effectiveness and efficiency of the police service.
(ii)   The consequences of police stress may have an adverse effect on the development and maintenance of good police relations with the public.
(iii)   There exists the possibility that police officers under stress can, in certain situations, constitute a real threat to their own safety, that of their fellow officers, the offenders they deal with and indeed the general public.

A further reason for special concern is the long-term maintenance of police numbers during the expected demographic decline in the number of young people available for employment in Britain. It is apparent that if the police service is to compete effectively with the commercial and other sectors to recruit and retain personnel in the future, it must be able to offer comparable benefits in the area of employee health and welfare.

Manolias's rationale provides a stronger case for supporting organisational stress intervention programmes for police officers than for developing a hypothesis about the vulnerability of police personality types.

Police Work Will Become even more Stressful in the Future

Fears have been expressed within the police service that society is becoming more violent and intolerant, the media more hostile, and the laws and procedures with which the police have to work more numerous and complicated (Reiner 1991). A number of future forecasts predict increases in racial tensions, terrorism and social problems (Operational Policing Review 1990; Tafoya 1986). The Operational Policing Review (1990) suggested that if economic strictures continued and the recession deepened, the police would be called upon with greater frequency to deal with the elderly and mentally disturbed. It also predicted that there would be increased problems deriving from ethnic clashes and drugs-related crime. Tafoya (1986), using the Delphi technique in which experts move towards some consensus view, predicted that in the United States there would be an increase in the volume of violent and property crime, computer crime, terrorism, and urban unrest due to economic inequities. Tafoya concludes that new policing priorities must be accompanied by changes in management style if the challenges presented are to be met.

The police are there to deal with problems created by society itself. Yet many feel it has become unclear whether they are being used as a *force* or a *service*, or indeed whether their responsibilities have any clear limits. It has been suggested that stress in the police is increasing as they take on more and more of the responsibilities of the rest of society, and that the police are increasingly being asked to deal with the effects of high unemployment, political tension, and social deprivation whose causes more appropriately may be the province of politicians and social planners. If this increased police workload is both realised and becomes a source of police stress, then solutions could involve changing the role of the police service in society with aspects of policing becoming the joint responsibility of multiple groups within the community.

In summary then, the fact that police officers are exposed to sources of stress should be sufficient grounds to encourage management recognition of the need for support, if for nothing other than organisational self-interest in maintaining an efficient and effective public service. Further, given the role that police officers play in society presently, and anticipating possible future societal tensions, then the preservation of balanced police–public relationships should not be jeopardised by officers being unduly stressed. The next logical step then is to examine the available evidence purporting to demonstrate the types of stress the police are subject to, and the consequences for officers and the organisation.

EVALUATING THE EVIDENCE

Empirical evidence which could throw some light on the questions posed above is both hard to come by and often problematic to interpret. Although some research has indeed shown that the police tend to exhibit higher rates of stress-related disease, higher suicide rates and higher divorce rates (Somodevilla 1978), there are many difficulties with the data.

Much of the research on the effects of stress in the police has been carried out in the USA. The relevance of US results to the UK police force is questionable. Differences in cultural setting, age and gender composition, physical fitness, specific police roles as well as the policy on firearms may render many comparisons meaningless. For example, observation of high police suicide rates in the United States might not necessarily be taken as indicating that police in the United Kingdom should show similarly high rates.

Empirical work carried out on British police is sparse, and mostly has had small samples with limited sampling by rank and specialities of officers. Given the size and diversity of today's police forces, it is difficult to construct a reliable general picture from the available research.

General comparisons with other occupational groups are also problematic because the available empirical data on stress in different groups are not usually of the same type, of similar sample composition or even synchronous. Often they take no account of the different backgrounds and predispositions to stress of people choosing different kinds of work. Therefore claims that police officers suffer more stress than other occupational groups or that findings from other occupational environments can be generalised to the police must be treated with some caution.

Inferences from data based on other emergency services on the assumption of similarities are inadvisable for the same reasons. Strictly speaking, the results of an investigation on, for example, the sources of stress in fire fighters and nurses cannot be used as proxy data for the police. As Davidson and Veno (1980) have observed, given the special nature of the police service, the problems of occupational stress as they relate to the police must be investigated in the context in which they occur. The police tend to have a greater diversity of tasks than, say, ambulance crews or fire fighters.

When the police themselves were asked to list significant causes of stress they nominated the same occupational features which are associated with stress in the working lives of other kinds of employees. Officers from both the United States and the United Kingdom listed poor and insensitive supervision, unreasonable workload, shift work, personal safety and volume of paperwork as the most significant sources of stress at work (Kroes 1982; Brown and Campbell 1990). The report entitled *Stress in the Police Service* (Association of Chief Police Officers 1984) suggested that stress could be mostly attributed to management and organisational factors, a view reiterated by a House of Commons Home Affairs Committee (1991). However, such reports are neither always the product of systematic analysis nor do they employ precise definitions.

DEFINITIONS OF STRESS

There is no single agreed definition of stress. In the literature, the term covers a variety of different meanings according to the purposes of various writers. Three distinct approaches to the definition of stress can be identified.

In the first approach stress is defined as a stimulus variable. According to this model, stress is something that is imposed on a person from outside, ie external factors which bring about some degree of physical or psychological discomfort. In this model stress is caused by extremes of stimulation, either too much or too little.

In the second approach stress is defined as a response variable. This model, based on Selye's General Adaptation Syndrome (Selye 1956), views stress as a response process:

- *The initial alarm reaction.* The "fight or flight" response, which occurs when the person is exposed to frightening or threatening stimuli. The initial response includes physiological changes preparing the body for "fight or flight".
- *The stage of resistance.* The period during which the person adapts to external stressors and symptoms of stress improve or disappear.
- *The stage of exhaustion.* This follows if the stressor is sufficiently severe or prolonged. The person can no longer adapt, symptoms reappear and the end result is death.

Stress is thus thought to be the result of irreversible physical changes associated with unsatisfied, continuous "fight or flight" response which eventually lead to illness and death when the body is no longer able to adapt.

In the third approach stress is defined as an interactive variable. This third model allows for individual differences in response to potentially stressful situations. It suggests that situations are not stressful in themselves, but that stress results from an imbalance between perceived environmental demands on the individual and his or her perceived response capability. That is, situations become stressful or distressing when individuals believe they cannot cope with the demands of their environment, the emphasis being on an individual's perception of the situation.

It is apparent that stress is highly complex, interactive and can be highly individual in nature. Most discussions of stress focus on its negative effects in terms of health, well-being and productivity. For the purposes of this book three elements are distinguished:

(i)   *Stressors* which are potential external sources of adverse reactions.

(ii)   *Stress* defined as self-perceived negative impact (felt stress).
(iii)   *Distress* being reserved for the experience of specific out-
        comes such as physical or psychological symptoms or prob-
        lems.

MEASUREMENT OF STRESS, STRESSORS AND DISTRESS

The measurement of stress is also complex. This is partly because
of the difficulty involved in attributing specific outcomes to specific causes, ie the vagueness of the causal route. The effects of
stress are many and varied and as such the way in which they are
measured depends to a certain extent on the purposes of measurement (cf Hockey 1983; Kasl and Cooper 1987; Fisher and Reason
1988).

Stress affects individuals at all levels of functioning from the
physiological to the behavioural. The effects of stress involve
changes of a physical, psychological and/or a behavioural nature.
Changes at any one level are inextricably linked with changes at
other levels. It is possible, for example, to measure physiological
changes (such as alterations in heart-rate, blood pressure or hor-
mone secretion), psychological changes (such as anxiety or irritability) or behavioural changes (such as changes in smoking, drinking, eating and medication habits). Techniques of measurement
range from laboratory measures of galvanic skin response and
hormonal assay of urine samples to "gross" measures such as rates
of alcoholism, absenteeism and suicide. Frequently, investigators
seek the self-reported responses from population samples thought
to be subject to stress. Here, inventories of postulated sources of
stress are devised and various types of adverse physical or
psychological consequences measured: eg coronary heart disease,
anxiety, depression, somatic symptoms, social dysfunction. It is
obvious that the unit chosen for the measurement of stress or
distress is to a large extent dependent on the purpose of the study
and the resources available.

Laboratory studies present both practical and methodological
problems in the collection of urine and/or blood samples (Evans
and Cohen 1987). Techniques to collect samples are invasive or

intrusive, baseline measurement must be established, individual differences accounted for and care taken in the extrapolation of findings to the real world context from which they are drawn.

The use of "gross" measures of the ultimate effects of stress on health and behaviour has a number of practical advantages. First, individuals may be generally unaware of the underlying physiological changes associated with stress until they are manifested as symptoms, ie as changes in health, emotional feelings, or motivation. Data based on these measures may already be available to researchers in the form of sickness absence records and other routinely collected statistics. However, these "gross" measures must be used with caution since they tend to apply to groups rather than individuals and there is not a one-to-one relationship between a specific stressor and a particular outcome measure.

Multi-modal measurement represents the most complete approach in studies of adverse consequences but such studies tend to be rare because of time and resource constraints and the complexity of collecting and cross-referencing data.

A detailed critique of stress inventories and psychometric techniques is beyond the scope of this volume (cf Kasl and Cooper 1987). As mentioned earlier, some pitfalls can be avoided if an explicit model is followed when attempting to measure the three separate but interrelated factors: "stressors" and "felt stress" and "distress".

SYMPTOMS OF STRESS

Stress has been demonstrated to impair the social, psychological and physical functioning of the individual. On the whole, stressed individuals are more likely to experience job dissatisfaction, decreased productivity, increased rates of error and accidents, poor judgement, and delayed reaction times. Psychological changes such as increased irritability, anxiety, tension, feeling "uptight" or "flying off the handle" can affect working relationships with colleagues. Another effect of stress is to depress the immune system so that stressed individuals are more susceptible to disease and thereby more likely to be absent from work. This implies a period of reduced work effectiveness before and after illness, as well as increasing the stress loads on staff having to compensate for the absent officer.

Continued stress may result in undesirable behaviour changes, such as drug dependency, substance abuse (usually alcoholism), work absenteeism, and it may also increase the likelihood of marital breakdown and suicide. Long-term effects of stress include chronic disease such as high blood pressure, heart disease, diabetes and asthma attacks. These can result in early retirement on health grounds and, in extreme cases, in premature mortality. As well as emotional costs to the individual and to surviving family members they also incur financial costs in terms of recruiting and training replacements.

The concept of stress is conceptually complex and methodologically problematic. Confusion is likely if it is not made clear at the outset what the term has been taken to mean. The most important points to be made here are:

(i)   that "stress", however defined, is inextricably linked with all aspects of an individual's existence;
(ii)   that the definition of stress will usually depend on the purpose of the enquiry, and in turn on the method used to measure it;
(iii)   that it can be measured in many different ways;
(iv)   that it is often most practical and useful for developing policy to measure stress in terms of its impacts.

MODELLING STRESS IN POLICE WORK

For the present text, as has been mentioned previously, distinctions are made between stressors, felt stress and distress. Thus stressors are the potential external sources of adverse individual reactions. It is recognised that some stressors may result in positive reactions such as excitement when engaged in a high speed car chase. However, for the purposes of the elaboration here, it is the adverse reactions which are of interest. Identification of the sources of occupational stress is now relatively sophisticated with broad dimensions of intraindividual, organisational and extra-organisational factors appearing in many analyses (Cooper 1986). Felt stress is the degree to which individuals ascribe experiences as being stressful to them. This is the self-report and/or perceived adverse effects of being exposed to a stressor. Clearly the notion of individual differences plays a part here. Davidson and Veno (1980) note that whilst reviewing aspects of stress it is important to take into account the individual's responses to adverse situations. This in turn has been associated with personality, and life experiences, as well as variables such as age, gender and family history.

Distress is the experience of physical or psychological symptoms as a consequence of exposure to adverse circumstances. Most properly these are subject to some external assessment by investigators and externally verified.

It is possible to map the various factors of interest and their interrelationships in predicting the likelihood of police officers being exposed and responding adversely to stressors through a device called a mapping sentence. This technique is derived from the theoretical orientation of Louis Guttman, summarised in Brown (1985). A mapping sentence is a linguistic device for defining the universe of observations and specifying their hypothesised interrelationships. For present purposes then, the mapping sentence defining the variables of interest in police officers' experience of adverse reactions to occupational stressors is given in Table 2.

In other words, any exposition of the concept of occupational stress within the police must define stressors from sources within the broad classes of operational activities, organisational and management features of the police service, and external factors impinging on their occupational lives. Exposure to these, and adverse consequences arising from exposure, is postulated to be associated with aspects of the individual him or herself, for example personality, demographic characterisation and occupational profile, eg rank or post held. Both exposure to and suffering from adverse consequences of stressors are postulated to be functions of these defining characteristics.

Table 2.   Mapping sentence modelling stress in police work

The likelihood of police officers being exposed to:

$$\left\{ \begin{array}{l} \text{operational} \\ \text{organisational} \\ \text{management or} \\ \text{extra-organisational} \end{array} \right\} \quad \text{stressors}$$

$$\left\{ \begin{array}{l} \text{reporting} \\ \text{not reporting} \end{array} \right\} \quad \text{felt stress and/or}$$

$$\left\{ \begin{array}{l} \text{reporting} \\ \text{not reporting} \end{array} \right\} \quad \text{psychological/physical symptoms}$$

$$\text{is a function of} \quad \left\{ \begin{array}{l} \text{individual} \\ \text{demographic} \\ \text{occupational} \end{array} \right\} \quad \text{characteristics}$$

$$\text{varies from} \quad \left\{ \begin{array}{c} \text{very likely} \\ \text{to} \\ \text{very unlikely} \end{array} \right\}$$

Source: reproduced by permission from J. M. Brown and E. A. Campbell, Sources of occupational stress in the police. *Work and Stress*, **4**, 305–318.

SUMMARY AND PLAN OF THE BOOK

The subject of stress has been brought to the attention of policy-makers by a mixture of political forces, lobbying and chance events. Humanitarian concerns and those of finance and organisational effectiveness have converged. Identifying appropriate stress-reduction strategies will depend in part on the strength of the available evidence to demonstrate the severity of impact of stressors.

Despite the uncertainty of demonstrable and reliable evidence of the specific experience of police officers and their exposure to stressors, there is compelling evidence from other occupational groups that stress-related symptoms do result in significant per-formance and productivity losses. Thus the police, in common with other organisations, have begun to tackle these problems.

Considerable research effort has been put into the study of traumatic incidents (Hillas and Cox 1986; Duckworth 1986, 1987) but less so into the more routine operational police stressors. One study which has addressed the role of such stressors as answering a call for assistance from an officer, attending the scene of sudden death, dealing with victims of sexual abuse, or arresting a violent person, is that of Brown and Campbell (1990). These stressors reflect the front line responsibility for social emergencies and vulnerability to violence that police officers are exposed to, as highlighted by Callan (1989). The following chapters seek to expand and clarify the sources and consequences of stress and to present some practical solutions in relation to the nature of the problem of stress within the police service.

Chapter 2 begins by examining the sources of routine stressors to which the police are exposed. A four-way classification is suggested that defines the broad types of stressor. These are features that firstly are general to organisations and reflect the internal management procedures and systems within the police, and secondly are aspects of the external world but still impinge on organisations at large, eg relationship with groups in the community. Special features internal to the police, which include front line policing duties, represent the third type of stressor, whilst the final type are constituted by special features of policing but relate to other institutional contexts such as the courts or other emergency services. Details are presented outlining examples of stressors within these four broad types and assessment is made of the available evidence. Chapter 3 explores in detail traumatic incident stress, as a special case stressor, and consequent Post Traumatic Stress Disorder (PTSD). Three broad types of traumatic incident are defined: criminal injury or violence, accidents, and public disorder. The consequences of exposure to such incidents are described, as are the difficulties experienced by the individual, police managers and professional practitioners in acknowledging PTSD. Risk factors are elaborated in identifying vulnerable officers and suggestions made for helping officers following their exposure to traumatic incidents.

Chapter 4 discusses the consequences of exposure to stressors in terms of impaired job performance, psychological problems and physical health problems. Attention is paid to absenteeism in particular, as well as to depression, anxiety and alcohol abuse as the most likely psychological consequences associated with stress. Physical ill-health and injury are included in the chapter as is a discussion on mortality rates of police officers. Factors thought to be especially associated with stress—location, rank, role, personality type, and behaviour patterns—are also discussed and evaluated.

Chapter 5 analyses different subgroups within the police organisation and identifies stressors associated with these. Thus differences in exposure to and impact of stressors experienced by junior and more senior officers are described. The experiences of women officers, ethnic minority officers and homosexual officers are documented. There is also a section on the stressors affecting civilian or non-sworn personnel who work for the police.

The next two chapters explore possible solutions to the problems created by stressors. The focus of Chapter 6 is the individual and it addresses the question of the efficacy of self-help methods to alleviate stress symptoms. Various forms of counselling are described, as are stress management programmes, including physical fitness. Organisational and management practices are the focus of Chapter 7 and three areas are looked at in some detail: personnel practices, training, and communication. These tend to represent intermediate timescale preventive measures.

Chapter 8 presents an analysis of the cultural context of policing. The proposition that the organisation itself is a source of stress is discussed, as are attempts to change the structure and culture of the police service. Such attempts are necessarily long-term strategies which may eventually have beneficial effects on the management style and practices of the organisation, which in turn is likely to improve the health and psychological well-being of individuals. Some assessment is presented of the impact and influence of different groups within the police service such as women officers or those entering having achieved qualifications at tertiary level education.

The final chapter presents a summary and overview together with some pointers for individuals and police managers to avoid or alleviate occupational stress.

CHAPTER 2

Routine Stressors

There have been many attempts to distinguish the sources of stress to which police officers may be exposed (Davidson and Veno 1980; Robinson 1981; Violanti and Marshall 1983; Cacioppe and Mock 1985; Gudjonsson and Adlam 1985; Martelli, Waters and Martelli 1989; Brown and Campbell 1990). These attempts range from itemising specific stressors or defining broad categories to proposing models linking sources with consequences of stress. For the purposes of this chapter, sources of stress are confined to those that are routinely occupationally generated. Features relating to intraindividual aspects of stress are dealt with in the section on mediating influences in Chapter 4 whilst the rarer traumatic incidents are the subject of Chapter 3.

UNDERLYING DIMENSIONS

Two axes underpin much of the research identifying possible sources of stress that may routinely and potentially impinge on police officers. These are features that are generic to organisations and those that are specific (but not necessarily unique) to the police; and features that are internal to the Police Service and those that are external to it. These distinctions drawn by earlier investigators (Symonds 1970; Eisenberg 1975; Kroes, Margolis and Hurrel 1974; Kroes 1976; Ellison and Genz 1983) can be illustrated in Table 3.

These broad categories feature in much of the subsequent work exploring sources of stress. They will be used as a framework to present available evidence on the status of specific items subsumed under these broad headings.

Table 3. Sources of routinely occurring stressors

	Internal to the police	External to the police
Generic features	Aspects of the organisation and management	Community relations
Specific features	Operational police tasks	Interaction with criminal justice system

GENERIC FEATURES WITHIN THE ORGANISATION

Research on sources of occupational stress identifies common features occurring within many organisational settings that have to do with working methods and styles of management (Cooper 1986; Glowinkowski and Cooper 1985). In a study of occupational stress in a British police force, Brown and Campbell (1990) identified the most frequently reported organisational and management stressors (Table 4). The research relating to some of these stressors is reviewed below.

Table 4. Reported exposure rate to organisational and management stressors in a sample of British police officers

	Officers of all ranks (%)
Staff and manpower shortages	72
Shift work	68
Working with civilians	60
Time pressures	57
Lack of consultation/communication	52
Managing and supervising people	49
Long hours	49
Work overload	48
Inadequate resources/finance	44
Demands of work impinging on home	44

Source: compiled from Brown and Campbell (1990).

Shift Work

Numerous studies have reported shift work to be a major job stressor (eg Monk 1988; Rosa, Colligan and Lewis 1989). There has been limited empirical support for an association between stress-related symptoms amongst police officers and shift work (Davidson and Veno 1980). Whilst rotating shift work is reported as a source of stress in surveys of police officers, Davidson and Veno (1980) point out that shift workers do habituate and can accommodate their social lives within shift regimes. Recent interest in the eponymous Ottawa Shift pattern would suggest that, because this shift pattern allows a mini break of six days between change-over from different shifts and also because the pattern follows a delayed rotation, ie mornings, afternoons and nights, it is both preferred and potentially less stressful. A small-scale study of the self-reported stress associated with the Ottawa System was conducted on 51 officers participating in an experimental scheme at a British police station (Cullen 1989). No measurable differences were found in participants' symptom scores before the introduction of the new shift system and nine months later. Symptoms were measured using the General Health Questionnaire (28 item version). This is a well established questionnaire devised to assess the rate of probable psychological distress in a population (Goldberg 1978). Whilst there were no reported differences in the GHQ scores, there was a statistically significant difference in the rate at which shift work was identified as a self-perceived source of stress with rates declining after the introduction of the Ottawa shift pattern (Cullen 1989).

These results, however, may reflect the investment of the police officers to demonstrate the efficacy of the Ottawa Shift, which emerged as their preferred working pattern rather than any improvement engendered by this shift arrangement per se. An evaluation of 19 forces using the Ottawa shift pattern and five forces operating an orthodox police regulation shift included an officer perception inventory (Touche Ross 1992). While the authors admit that there were limitations to their measures, the 277 respondents participating in the trials indicated increased satisfaction in well-being in personal, social and family life. Ottawa Shift officers were more likely to take exercise and report improved sleeping patterns. However, there are some anomalies in the data. For example, pre-Ottawa and regulation shift officers showed differences in personal and family domains, with the Ottawa officers reporting higher rates of satisfaction even before starting their new shift.

In part this may be explained by respondents having to recall levels of satisfaction before undertaking the new shift as questionnaires were completed retrospectively.

The balance of available evidence suggesting that police officers suffer stress or distress as a result of shift work is limited, although as Brown and Campbell (1990) report, most police officers indicate that shift work is a self-identified source of stress.

Job Overload

Overload has been described as having too much to do and/or things being too difficult (French and Caplan 1972). Personnel shortages and long working hours are frequently cited as potential sources of stress in American and Australian police forces (Davidson and Veno 1980). Brown and Campbell (1990) found staff shortages and time pressures and deadlines amongst the most frequently cited stressors resulting in self-perceived stress in their study of police officers serving in a large English provincial force. Work overload per se was mentioned as occurring by 48% of the sample. Of these 67% reported that overload was experienced as stressful.

Cooper, Davidson and Robinson (1982) report results from a study of 191 police officers from a large Metropolitan British police force. Job overload emerged as a significant factor in regression analyses predicting psychological ill-health as measured by the Middlesex Hospital Questionnaire (MHQ). However, some caution must be exercised in interpreting these results as analyses were conducted on small groups of officers, and the questionnaire did not indicate whether officers had actually been personally exposed to sources of stress.

Gudjonsson and Adlam (1985) found in their study of British police probationer constables (N = 75), sergeants (N = 33) and senior officers (N = 79) that nearly all indicated that they experienced excessive paperwork but the stressfulness associated with this was relatively low. On the one hand paperwork is more likely to be seen as a frustration, contrasting with the situations of high activity and excitement that generated the paperwork in the first place. On the other hand, there is some evidence (Highmore 1989) that detectives find a level of job satisfaction in putting together complicated case files. Davidson and Veno (1980) found that excessive paperwork was cited as a potential source of stress but claim that its relative contribution to actual symptoms is not established amongst police officers.

In a study conducted by Brown, Cooper and Dudman (1992) police chief superintendents and superintendents cited "having too much work to do", as being the most likely source of stress. The top ten ranking of routine stressors by these senior officers is shown in Table 5.

Table 5. Most frequently cited sources of routine stressors for British police chief superintendents and superintendents

1. Having too much work to do
2. Staff shortages and unsettling turnover rate
3. Insufficient finance or resources
4. Lack of consultation or communication
5. Mundane administrative tasks or paperwork
6. Factors not under your direct control
7. Characteristics of the organisation's structure
8. Attending meetings
9. Keeping up with new techniques
10. Misuse of time by other people

Source: Brown, Cooper and Dudman (1992).

Equipment

Davidson and Veno (1980) report relatively high levels of dissatisfaction amongst American and Australian police officers with the standard of equipment available to them. Having to deal with new equipment, especially that associated with information technology, has emerged as a potential source of stress in the British police for some officers. Brown and Campbell (1990) found 30% of their sample reported being exposed to this, of whom 29% reported being stressed by it.

In a study of a large provincial English police force's control rooms, Chadwick, Hill, Highmore and Brown (1989) found that of the 233 staff completing a stressor inventory, 80% reported being exposed to equipment breakdown or failure. Of these, 90% reported feeling stressed by this. Apart from self-attributed stress associated with staffing shortages and lack of resources to deal with incidents, equipment problems within the control rooms were associated with the highest levels of felt stress. In a comparable study (N = 226) of a large English metropolitan force police and civilian control room staff, 61% reported experiencing equipment breakdown, of whom 72% indicated a degree of associated stress (Funnelle, Brown and Woolfendon 1991). Sewell and Crew (1984) noted that equipment failures were a significant source of stress amongst civilian dispatchers working in US Police Communications centres. However, none of these studies had independent measures of adverse outcomes such as sickness absence rates or physiological manifestations of stress.

Role-based Stress

Police officers face a number of potential role conflicts and role ambiguities. By this is meant that there are a number of possible conflicting demands that can be made on them by the job and by their families. Sources of role conflict relate to the tensions experienced as officers move through their occupational socialisation learning the values and orientation of the organisation (Van Mannen and Schein 1979). Fielding (1987) has studied the anxieties experienced by probationer constables in a study of approximately 100 recruits in a British police force. This revealed a number of key points in the training particularly stressful to recruits. The most notable stressor was the first experience of beat work.

Brown and Campbell (1990) found that 30% of officers in their study indicated that they experienced conflicting demands between their work and home lives. Nearly all of these (92%) found this conflict of demands to be stressful. Gudjonsson and Adlam (1985) reported that 67% of probationers, 70% of sergeants and 82% of senior officers experienced role ambiguity although the relative stress rating attached to this source of stress was modest.

There has been some discussion in the literature of a more global crisis of role identity among the British police (Reiner 1991). This discussion suggests that there is a lack of clarity about the role and purpose of the police exemplified by two extreme pictures of the British police officer—the bobby on the beat exercising individual discretion and as a member of a riot squad functioning as a paramilitary officer (Operational Policing Review 1990). In Britain, the same officers may be required to perform both roles. There is no explicit evidence to demonstrate that flipping from community policing to riot control is a source of stress in itself. There is, however, an indication that exposure to public order duties is stressful (Gudjonsson and Adlam 1985). Such discussions are not limited to the British police. In Chapter 8, similar dilemmas are discussed as they relate to public order and community policing in the United States brought into focus by the Los Angeles Police Department's experiences.

Relationships at Work

In a series of workshop studies in which police delegates from five British police forces discussed sources of stress, Manolias (1983) identified management style as a significant factor. By this was meant the way in which police supervisors control their subordinates. It was suggested that poor management such as excessive attention to detail, lack of communication, poor consultation, fault finding and lack of concern for individuals contributed to police officer stress. More particularly, infrastructures underpinning management support were found to be lacking.

The quality of relationships between colleagues and between superior and subordinate officers, as well as with other members of the police organisations, is implicated as a source of reported stress (Davidson and Veno 1980). American and Australian studies indicate that a majority of respondents reported a lack of social support and poor communication from their police supervisors.

There is evidence from available British studies that confirms the contention that lack of support and poor communication are experienced by police officers as stressful (Robinson 1981; Gudjonsson and Adlam 1985; Brown and Campbell 1990). Autocratic management and lack of consultation, or insufficient interaction with decision-makers were found to contribute to the psychological distress of police officers in Cooper, Davidson and Robinson's (1982) study of a British Metropolitan police force.

Career Development Factors

Glowinkowski and Cooper (1985) draw attention to career development research which suggests that sources of stress are related to career progression—ie establishment, advancement and maintenance stages. The early stages of a police career are marked by probationer training which in Britain lasts two years. As has been previously mentioned, Fielding (1987) found particular anxieties related to this stage. During the advancement stage promotion concerns dominate. Davidson and Veno (1980) reviewed evidence to suggest that limitations on promotion opportunities and career mobility present two significant sources of occupational stress in the police both in America and in Australia. Silvester (1989) found that a significant reason for the premature retirement of British graduate police officers was their frustration through lack of promotion.

At the maintenance stage, different factors appear to operate. Fear of obsolescence or even negative attitudes to the organisation may now dominate. Glowinkowski and Nicholson (1984) found that middle-aged British police inspectors held very negative attitudes towards the organisation in terms of their own careers. It was perceived as a reward system, and lack of further promotion was associated with a series of superstitious beliefs and feelings of uncertainty. Brown and Campbell (1990) found in their study that 18% of the total sample believed they were underpromoted whilst half of the 14% who recently had had promotion boards found this stressful.

There is increasing evidence to show that the behaviour of the police officer is related to the style and goals adopted by the managers of police organisations. Recent studies have shown that the values, rank and formal structures of the police organisation relate to the feelings of work satisfaction or alienation that are experienced by the individual officer. Such a study carried out in one police organisation by Wagoner (1976) concluded that:

> there is a direct relationship between the amount of formality in the organisation and alienation (lack of commitment to organisational goals and beliefs); there is a direct relationship between the degree of formality and the breaking of organisational rules to achieve goals in those of lower ranks, and there is considerably more alienation/ powerlessness among those officers with less control over decisions in their job.

Sexual Harassment

There is a growing body of research which suggests sexual harassment at work is a significant source of stress for women in general (Gutek 1985; Rubenstein 1988; Stockdale 1991) and policewomen in particular (Kroes 1982; Wexler and Logan 1983). Defining this as unwanted and unreciprocated behaviour with a sexual dimension (Rubenstein 1988), research investigators have demonstrated negative consequences amongst university student populations (Malovich and Stake 1990); nurses (Grieco 1987); and autoworkers (Maypole and Skaine 1982). Consequences are described as decreased work satisfaction (Kissman 1990) and psychological trauma (Mezey and Rubenstein 1992). Whilst not unique to the police, sexual harassment may be especially prevalent within such an obviously male-dominated organisation. Gutek (1985) proposed that gender-based role expectations spill over into the workplace. Women are assumed to be passive, loyal, emotionally nurturant and sexually responsive to overtures from men. Where the sex ratio of an occupation is significantly skewed, as in the police, there is more likelihood that sexual pursuits will be seen as competitive male horseplay. Researchers examining sources of stress amongst policewomen find sexual harassment amongst the most often cited sources of stress (Kroes 1982; Wexler and Logan 1983). This issue is explored in further detail in the next chapter.

POLICE SPECIFIC STRESSORS

Physical Danger

Much of the early American literature identifies physical dangers associated with police work (Lewis 1973; Reiser 1974, 1976; Kroes, Margolis and Hurrel 1974). Davidson and Veno (1980) review this literature as follows:

> According to Kroes (1976), physical danger—which can result from line of duty/crisis situations between minority group members, in which a threat to an officer's physical well-being may overwhelm him emotionally—is a specific police stressor not shared by any other occupational groups. While we support Eisenberg's (1975) claim that danger, fear of serious injury and disability, and even death can make police work a hazardous environment in which to work and are probably major job stressors, we cannot agree with Kroes' assumption that such conditions are unique to police careers. Kasl (1973), for instance, isolates other occupations which share similar physical dangers as including mine workers, soldiers, and firemen.

Exposure to violence has been linked to felt stress among nurses, teachers and social workers as well as police officers (Health Education Authority 1988). Two factors must complicate any assessment of the violence/stress relationship. First, the risk of violence is not evenly spread within an occupation: among nurses for example it is apparently concentrated among casualty staff. Second, perceptions of violence (as distinct from its actual incidence) may be influenced by many factors including the overall world-view prevalent within an occupation, within society at large, and within the political arena. Young (1984) argues that police perceptions of vulnerability to violence are part of a coherent belief system that emphasises "the rising tide of violence in society". Such perceptions are in turn used for ideological purposes such as sustaining a definition of "real", ie tough, police work. Jermier, Gaines and McIntosh (1989) discuss this issue at some length and their observations are referred to in detail in Chapter 7. However, an important aspect highlighted by them is the notion of the anticipation of danger, which they argue is crucial in the maintenance of male police officers' "macho" identity.

Front Line Duties

Of the actual operational duties that police officers indicated as sources of stress in the Brown and Campbell (1990) study, arresting a violent person was experienced by 50% of officers, 60% of whom reported this as stressful. Table 6 gives the proportions of officers of all ranks who had been exposed to specific operational stressors in the previous six months. The probationer constables were most likely to be exposed to this, with the exposure rate diminishing with increasing seniority of officer, as illustrated in Table 7. This trend was also observed by Gudjonsson and Adlam (1985).

Table 6. Reported exposure rates to operational policing stressors in a sample of British police officers

	Officers of all ranks (%)
Attending scene of a sudden death	58
Arresting violent person	50
Dealing with victims of violence	38
Informing relatives of a sudden death	37
Search for a missing person	37
Answering call for officer assistance	35
Appearing as a witness at Crown Court	34
Football duty	31
Dealing with victims of sexual offence	25
Attending large-scale public order event	21

Source: Brown and Forde (1989).

There is generally a dearth of evidence to support the proposition that front line duties which form the routine part of police activities contribute to either perceived stress or symptoms of distress. It is important here to distinguish between routine operational stressors and traumatic incidents, which are the subject of Chapter 3.

Table 7. Reported exposure rates to most frequently occurring operational policing stressors by rank of officer

	Proba- tioner (%)	PC (%)	Sgt (%)	Insp (%)	Chief Insp (%)	Supt & higher ranks (%)
Attending sudden death	83	65	50	51	24	12
Arresting a violent person	62	57	49	39	27	15
Dealing with victim of violence	40	40	41	36	15	12
Informing relatives of sudden death	43	48	30	18	2	3
Searching for missing person	51	41	31	34	24	12
Answering call for officer	43	40	29	31	17	6
Appearing as a witness at Crown Court	77	39	32	29	22	21
Football duty	23	35	27	36	20	18
Dealing with victim of sexual offence	40	29	21	17	12	9
Public order event	23	24	17	19	15	12

Source: Brown and Forde (1989).

Work by Gudjonsson and Adlam (1983) found that a national sample of British police officers rated as "very stressful" the following situations: being taken as a hostage; confronting a person with a gun; and a dangerous or violent confrontation. However, this study did not ask if the respondent had actually experienced these events. As Wagner (1986) points out, these are relatively rare and could be classified as traumatic events. More routine operational duties such as delivering messages about sudden deaths, dealing with domestic disturbances, being involved in a brawling incident, were associated with relatively lower levels of self-perceived stress. In a later study Gudjonsson and Adlam (1985) found that 67% of probationers had delivered a message about sudden death, compared to 42% of sergeants and

16% of more senior officers. They all report a relatively low level of stress associated with this. Brown and Campbell (1990) found 43% of their probationer sample had recently delivered a death message compared to 30% of sergeants and 18% of inspectors. Of those that did, most reported a moderate degree of felt stress associated with it. Of other operational duties itemised by Brown and Campbell, such as searching for a missing person, assisting a fellow officer in difficulty, supervising a football match, appearing as witness in court, fewer than a third of officers report these as stressful.

GENERIC EXTERNAL FEATURES

There are two aspects of the relationship with the community that have been identified as potential sources of stress for the police. These are exposure to media or public criticism and quality of police public relations. These latter are hypothesised to increase police alienation and subsequently increase stress (Davidson and Veno 1980).

Public Criticism

Eisenberg (1975) reports that a possible source of stress amongst American police officers is their perception of distorted press accounts of police incidents. This view holds that the press not only distorts its coverage, thus offending police officers, but such coverage also detracts from their public image.

In the United Kingdom, the most obvious profession to set alongside the police for comparison is that of social work (Fineman 1985). The comment attributed to a social worker (Health Education Authority 1988) that "If you don't do the right thing, society is ready to throw the book at you" would, it seems, reflect the anxieties of many police officers. Cases of child abuse and child deaths which became "media events" tended to be widely represented as "failures" of the social services and provided dramatic illustration of the sense of acute exposure experienced by social workers in sensitive areas when things do go wrong. For the police, it might be expected that a corresponding consciousness about public scrutiny is concentrated in areas of their work that are similarly socially sensitive, such as public order policing and community relations. That this sense of exposure is significant within the police service is suggested by the volume of research presently being conducted on pertinent topics. The British Police Foundation *Register of Policing Research* for 1986–7 listed six current projects on complaints (including one on "anti-police campaigns"), ten broadly directed to Community Relations and 21 on Public Order issues. Research has apparently not so far attempted to link exposure to public criticism with felt stress in any detailed way; this would clearly be a fruitful direction for further research. Meanwhile it is worth noting that behind the question of exposure to criticism lie two further clusters of concerns: concerns about *accountability* ("carrying the can" vis-à-vis the public when things go wrong) and concerns about *support* on the job (Fineman 1985). Hence the "exposure to criticism" variable converges with "frontline responsibility for social emergencies" and "ambiguities in the amount of permitted autonomy" (cf Karasek, Baker, Marxer, Ahlbom and Theorell 1981).

Quality of Police and Public Community Relations

Wilson (1968) suggested that in the United States there was a conflict between community demand for deterrence of criminal activities and police activities being directed towards service-orientated activities. This tension results in worsening of police–community relations. Kroes (1976) maintains that a negative public image represents a source of stress for police officers.

Whilst there is some evidence (Davidson and Veno 1980) of public dissatisfaction with the police, recent survey evidence from Britain shows a generally high level of satisfaction with them. However, research also shows that younger respondents and those from ethnic minorities (Operational Policing Review 1990), are amongst those sections of the community who are most likely to have negative attitudes towards the police.

The precise relationship between the experience of poor community relations with particular groups and the experience of stress is unclear. It may well be that those groups who have a negative view of the police are also amongst those groups towards whom the police themselves have negative attitudes. Thus police officers are likely to expect hostility from ethnic minorities or young people but whether this is a significant source of stress is not documented (Kinsey 1990).

POLICE SPECIFIC EXTERNAL FEATURES

Criminal Justice System

Kroes (1976) suggests that stressors associated with the judicial system are specific occupational stressors unique to police careers and not shared with other occupations. Most of the relevant research regarding this issue is North American. Choposky (1975), for instance, refers to earlier work by Kroes in which 50% of the police officers interviewed reported that they were bothered by the amount of time they had to spend in court and the general lack of consideration given in the scheduling of appearances; approximately 61% of Hurrel's (1977) US patrolmen complained of similar court-related inconveniences.

Eisenberg (1975) itemises as stressors for US police officers the ineffectiveness of correctional institutions in rehabilitating offenders, unfavourable court decisions, beliefs about the inefficiencies of the courts, and judicial delays.

Insufficient support from court officials and giving evidence in court were identified by Gudjonsson and Adlam (1985) as sources of stress for British police officers. Robinson (1981) also found police officers' frustration with the courts' treatment of offenders was a reported source of stress. Brown and Campbell (1990) found 34% of their sample had appeared in court as witnesses, but only 23% reported this as stressful. With regard to Australian cohorts, research by Wilson and Western (1972) indicated that 10% of time was taken up with court work in their police sample and 54% of Davidson's (1979) Northern Territories police respondents complained of frequent court delays.

Besides court appearances being time-consuming, police are often frustrated over judicial procedure, inefficiency, and court decisions (Eisenberg 1975; Margolis 1973). This was verified by Hurrel's (1977) and Davidson's (1979) American and Australian studies, both of which reported that approximately 86% of their police samples maintained that the courts were often too lenient with offenders.

SUMMARY

Much of the literature which attempts to identify likely sources of stress is not supported by empirical evidence. What empirical evidence there is is based on studies which often have small numbers of respondents, lack control or comparison groups, or use a great variety of measuring instruments such that any similarities in results are as likely to be due to methodological shortcomings as to inherent consistencies. Research on British police officers is rather meagre and there are problems in translating findings from country to country because of historical and cultural differences in the role of the police. Stress has been variously defined, and sources and outcomes often confused. Stress has also been used in a variety of ways to explain some operational failure, to glamorise or enhance the danger of the job or to emphasise the uniqueness of policing. Studies fail to report differences between self-perceived stressfulness of some incident or activity and some established link between symptoms and the experience of a stressor. Greller (1982) reports a study of 1638 officers from a large metropolitan police department in the United States. Perceived stress was distinguished from symptoms related to the exposure. Correlational analyses revealed an association between symptoms and management-generated stressors and between self-perceived stress and extra-departmental stressors. Greller concludes that there may be subcultural biases in reporting items that may be believed to be stressful and that an individual may not always have conscious access to the source of their stress and the severity of impact. This latter point is elaborated by Marmot and Madge (1987) who argue the need to employ a research design in which there is some independent assessment of the impact of stressful events on individuals, who may themselves through denial or misattribution incorrectly link the experience of a stressor with some stress outcome.

The preceding sections have reviewed evidence on the sources of stress impinging on police officers. There is clear support that shift work, job overload, manpower shortages, job underload, lack of equipment or equipment failures, role conflicts, lack of communication or consultation, career frustrations, and management styles are reported by police officers as being stressful to them. Physical danger, community relations, media criticisms and interaction with the criminal justice system also feature as likely sources of stress. Evidence from the subjective rating by police officers would seem to indicate that police operational duties are less often reported as sources of stress than the management and organisational features.

However, many studies do not employ multiple measurement of adverse outcomes and there is a problem in linking exposure to stressors and psychological or physical ill-health.

CHAPTER 3

Traumatic Incident Stress

Exposure to traumatic incidents is neither unique to police officers nor are officers known to be more exposed to such incidents than other services such as fire fighters and ambulance personnel, although hard evidence on this is difficult to come by. Nevertheless it has often been assumed that traumatic incidents constitute a major source of acute stress in the police service.

Generally speaking the importance of exposure to traumatic incidents as a major source of stress in the police service has been more widely recognised than the importance of stress resulting from routine police work. Traumatic incidents and Post Traumatic Stress Disorder (PTSD) in the police service have recently received considerable attention in both the United Kingdom and the United States. In the United Kingdom there has been a Joint Working Party on Organisational Health and Welfare which has reported on PTSD (Hillas and Cox 1986) and there has also been a report entitled "Post-shooting experiences in firearms officers" (Manolias and Hyatt-Williams 1986). Hillas and Cox (1986) point out that there are three main aspects to be considered by police forces in relation to traumatic incidents:

> (a) how the incidence of severely stressful situations and adverse reactions to them might be reduced, (b) how the organisation's immediate response might be developed to be more cathartic and supportive and (c) how the treatment and rehabilitation of officers might be made more effective.

Martin, McKean and Veltkamp (1986) report a study in which they distributed a questionnaire to police officers attending a crime seminar. Fifty-three officers (36% female) responded to the questionnaire, which asked about their experience of the various symptoms of PTSD following a job-related traumatic event. The traumatic events identified by this sample were: shooting someone; being shot; working with child abuse, spouse abuse and rape cases; being threatened or having one's family threatened; observing death through homicide, suicide or natural disaster.

Traumatic incidents associated with policing can therefore be divided into three broad types: criminal injury or violence to self or others; dealing with disasters, accidents, mutilations and fatalities; public disorder situations. Unfortunately there is virtually nothing written on the psychological reactions of police officers to public disorder situations. Therefore the following discussion will focus on injury or violence and disasters.

CRIMINAL INJURY AND VIOLENCE

A number of different types of events fall into this category:

(i)   shootings of or by the police officer;
(ii)   injury to the police officer while on duty because of criminal activity;
(iii)   dealing with victims of violent assault;
(iv)   narrowly escaping injury or death;
(v)   death or injury to a colleague at work;
(vi)   arresting a violent person.

Victims of Crime

Police officers often find themselves in situations where they believe, accurately or otherwise, that they are at risk of physical assault or injury. This may be in public order situations, one-to-one confrontations, or when in situations where they are possible terrorist targets. In this respect at least, police officers might be thought to have a different reaction to violent assault than other individuals. Young (1989) and other writers have described how one of the most striking effects of being a victim is the loss of the belief in a "just world". However, it is not clear whether police officers would share this psychological disruption since it might

be posited that they, by virtue of their occupation and its exposure
to crime and violence, would not have an assumption of a "just
world". There is no empirical evidence on this issue. It seems likely
that police officers do share the common view that there is an
underlying just world and that if they as individuals become
victims then they should show the same pattern of "why me?" and
loss of faith in the underpinnings of society. This reaction is part
of the intense emotional turmoil that victims often experience
(Davis and Friedman 1985; Kirsta 1988).

Police Officers as Victims

Assaults while on duty probably constitute the bulk of occasions
when police officers find themselves victims of violence. Figures
for 1989 compiled by the National Inspectorate of Police Forces for
England and Wales showed that more than 19 000 officers were
assaulted. This represented 14.9% of officers up to the rank of chief
inspector, ie those officers most likely to be exposed to situations
where they might be assaulted. In a study of one British police
force, Phillips and Cochrane (1991) also found a rate of 15% per
year for assaults while on duty. However, all of these figures need
to be treated with some caution because of intra- and interforce
variations in definitions of assault and in methods of recording
these. The House of Commons Home Affairs Committee (1991)
reported assault data for English and Welsh police forces and
noted considerable variation in the returns made by various police
forces. This Committee further cautioned that "the offence of
assault need not cause any injury. Spitting at an officer or roughly
pushing him or her are assaults. They are objectionable and
criminal conduct, but have little to do with police sickness." The
Committee also reported that assaults account for 3% of total days
lost through sickness absence.

Phillips and Cochrane (1991) found that, in the force they studied,
57% of assaults occurred between Friday night and Saturday
morning. Also nearly two-thirds of assaults overall occurred
during the night shift while only 7% occurred during the morning
shift. On the whole, younger and less experienced officers were
more at risk of assault, 90% being of constable rank. Women were
assaulted at a rate comparable to men, given the gender ratio.

Interestingly only 17% of assaults led to the officer taking sick leave. This study did not specifically address any psychological impact of assaults on officers.

The 1988 British Crime Survey found that police officers, prison officers, fire fighters and other security workers have at least three times the average risk of being victims of violent crime. In the United States, 78 police personnel were killed on duty in 1988 (Uniform Crime Reports 1988). In Britain relatively few officers are killed in the course of duty except in Northern Ireland where, since 1969, an average of ten officers per year have been murdered (Royal Ulster Constabulary 1992).

Shooting Incidents

The psychological impact on a police officer of wounding or killing another person in the course of their duties has been the focus of research interest in both North America and the United Kingdom (Stratton, Parker and Shibbe 1984; Loo 1986; Manolias and Hyatt-Williams 1986; Gersons 1989). In the Stratton, Parker and Shibbe (1984) study 60 North American police officers completed a questionnaire about their reactions to the shooting incidents in which they had been involved. The most commonly reported problems were flashbacks, sleep problems and a fear of legal proceedings. There was considerable variation in the reported emotional reaction to the shooting incidents. Just under one-third said that they were affected "greatly" or "a lot" by the incident, a further third said that they were moderately affected and 35% said that they were affected only a little or not at all. In a study of Canadian police officers, Loo (1986) found that the first three days following a shooting incident were the time of greatest psychological impact. Loo also notes that there was a considerable degree of variation in the time that officers reported it took them to get "back to normal". The average time was 20 weeks.

Manolias and Hyatt-Williams (1986) reported on a series of in-depth interviews with 25 British police officers who had been involved in shootings. They found that psychological symptoms most commonly included ruminations, sleeplessness, sudden waking, cold sweats and nightmares. Symptoms usually cleared up somewhere between several weeks and several months.

Anticipatory Anxiety: Fear of Crime or Assault

Most discussion of fear of crime has focused on the perception by certain members of the public that they are particularly at risk. These fears are often attributed to the elderly and to women. However, it is very likely that police officers themselves will suffer from a degree of fear of crime (Jermier, Gaines and McIntosh 1989). This will probably be linked both to the officer's prior exposure to violent crime or experience of personal assault and to their actual risk of being a victim in a particular posting.

One police force with a very high rate of death and injuries is the Royal Ulster Constabulary (RUC) in Northern Ireland. Brewer (1991) estimated that 1 in 16 members of that police force were killed or injured in the ten years up to August 1987. In his ethnographic study, Brewer (1991) found that police officers in the RUC had a variety of methods for dealing with their fear of death or injury. Officers were reluctant to express fear themselves but instead often claimed that their spouses and families were the fearful ones. Brewer (1991) also found that officers dealt with the ever present threat of political violence by the cognitive techniques of "normalisation" and "routinisation".

DISASTERS, ACCIDENTS AND FATALITIES

Disasters are usually divided into those that are natural and those that have some human agency behind them. Police officers are probably most likely to be exposed to transportation disasters of some kind (Kuch, Swinson and Kirby 1985; Hodgkinson 1988). Accidents are usually smaller scale incidents to which police officers may be routinely exposed. A number of features of accidents have been identified as being relevant to the psychological impact of accidents on rescue workers (Durham, McCammon and Allison 1985). These features include:

(i)   the extent, ie the number of people involved;
(ii)   the severity, ie whether there are fatalities or mutilations, whether children are involved;

(iii)   proximity, ie whether the officers have witnessed the event, whether officers themselves are victims of the incident.

Other fatalities that officers have to deal with are usually in the context of being called to the scene of "sudden deaths". As well as having to deal with the physical aspects of the scene, officers will often have to cope with the distress of witnesses or relatives. Anecdotally, police officers report that deaths of children, especially "unnecessary" or "avoidable" deaths such as cot deaths, are among the most difficult to deal with, both in terms of their own emotional reactions and also in dealing with the bereaveds' feelings.

There have been numerous accounts in the psychiatric literature of the impact of disasters on victims (Cohen and Ahearn 1980; Figley 1985,1986). However, apart from anecdotal reports of the impact on rescue workers, there is little in the way of empirical evidence about the psychological consequences of exposure to disasters for rescue personnel (Davidson 1979). Shepherd and Hodgkinson (1990) point out that those studies which have been undertaken on disaster rescue personnel have tended to be methodologically flawed. They attribute this in part to the practical difficulties involved in the need to respond quickly in studying disasters and also to the paucity of strong theories in this area. McCammon, Durham, Allison and Williamson (1988) surveyed police, fire, emergency medical and hospital personnel who were involved in two separate disasters in the United States. The first of these was an apartment building explosion and the second a series of tornadoes. These authors found that 14% of the personnel involved in the apartment explosion reported subsequent symptom patterns which corresponded to the criteria for Post Traumatic Stress Disorder; for the tornado personnel, the figure was 17%. Those personnel who had actually been present at the scene of the apartment disaster experienced greater degrees of distress than hospital personnel. However, there was no such difference between on-site personnel and hospital personnel following the tornado. The authors suggest that this may be due to the fact that the event was so overwhelming in scope that it had a similar impact on all those involved. Although if an event is sufficiently overwhelming and extensive almost all of those individuals exposed will suffer some degree of psychological distress, it is usually only a minority who would be diagnosed as suffering from the full syndrome of Post Traumatic Stress Disorder (PTSD). The standard definition of PTSD is that provided in the diagnostic manual compiled by the American Psychiatric Association (American Psychiatric Association 1987). The manual, DSM-III, gives the precise specification of the symptoms that are held to constitute PTSD. The term PTSD was first used in the edition of the manual published in 1980. The definition was then revised for the next edition of the manual published in 1987. Some of the symptoms seen in an individual with PTSD include: persistent and intrusive memories of the event; avoidance of feelings and situations associated with the event; loss of interest and feelings; difficulties in sleeping and concentrating; and hypervigilance. Although the term PTSD now has a wide circulation, it perhaps should be noted that there is still considerable debate in the professional journals about the status of the syndrome (Green, Lindy and Grace 1985; Mendelson 1987; March 1990).

Myers (1989) notes some issues related to characteristics of the event which may increase the stressfulness and thereby potentiate the risk of psychological problems in those exposed to it. The factors Myers lists are given in Table 8.

Brett and Ostroff (1985) list a number of factors that contribute to the difficulties that clinicians sometimes have in acknowledging Post Traumatic Stress Disorder in clients. These are listed in Table 9.

There have been very few studies which have looked specifically at police officers who have been involved in traumatic events. Duckworth and Charlesworth (1988) described various psychological aspects of the reactions of the police officers who were involved in the Bradford City football stadium fire disaster:

> It was observed that many of the police officers who had been involved in either the rescue or recovery phases of the incident were talkative, emotional and excitable: they had a positive urge to talk out and share their experiences amongst themselves and with others, and there was in many cases a marked reluctance to leave the incident and go home.

Table 8. Factors which increase the stressfulness of traumatic incidents or disasters

1. A lack of warning about the event

2. An abrupt contrast of scene

3. Technological disasters versus natural disasters because it is often assumed that these could have been prevented

4. The nature of the destructive agent, for example if the cause is familiar such as a regularly flooding river rather than an unfamiliar one such as chemicals or radiation

5. The degree of uncertainty and the duration of the threat. For example aftershocks following an earthquake make it difficult to know when safety has returned

6. Time of occurrence with events at night being worse than daylight events

7. Scope of the event: the more widespread the damage, injuries and death the greater the impact

8. Traumatic aspects such as involvement of children, prolonged contact with the dead, distressing sights, sounds or smells

9. Human error might be seen to have been preventable and therefore more distressing

10. Features of the post-disaster environment such as weather conditions, hazards, poor living conditions, frustrations

Source: adapted from D. G. Myers (1989). Mental health and disaster: Preventive approaches to intervention. In R. Gist and B. Lubin (Eds), *Psychological Aspects of Disaster*. Chichester: Wiley.

Duckworth (1986) surveyed all 399 officers who had been involved in any capacity with the disaster, sending them a screening questionnaire to complete. Counselling was then offered to officers who scored above a certain cut-off that was indicative of possible psychological problems. Between one and five counselling sessions were offered to those officers. Duckworth and Charlesworth (1988) identified five major problems that were common among the group of 34 officers who received counselling.

Table 9.   Factors which make recognition of PTSD difficult

1. Clients themselves often do not reveal the traumatic event

2. Some secondary disorder, such as alcohol or substance abuse, may be overlaid and "masking" the PTSD

3. The phenomenology of PTSD overlaps with that of other psychological disorders

4. Trauma associated imagery is misinterpreted as symptomatic of other conditions such as schizophrenia

Source: adapted from E. A. Brett and R. Ostroff (1985). Imagery and Post-Traumatic Stress Disorder: An overview. *American Journal of Psychiatry,* **142,** 417–424. Reproduced by permission of the American Psychiatric Association.

These problems were:

(i)   performance guilt: where an officer blamed him or herself for deaths or injuries;
(ii)   reconstruction anxiety: experienced when officers contemplated what *might* have happened to them;
(iii) focused resentment: the feeling that other people had done the "wrong" thing;
(iv)   generalised irritability: with family, friends and colleagues;
(v)   motivational changes: an inability to engage with a variety of tasks.

They recommend a number of things that might be taken into account for managing the human side of a disaster. In particular they suggest that there should be post-incident, ad hoc debriefings by supervisory officers who have been trained for that task. In addition, professional psychological help should be available for those officers who feel that they need it.

Martin, McKean and Veltkamp (1986) note that recurrent and intrusive recollection of the traumatic event was one of the most frequently reported symptoms in their sample of police officers who had either been exposed to working with victims or had been victims themselves. However, they also observed that police officers are likely to have repeated exposures to situations which are similar to the original trauma and they assume that this would exacerbate the occurrence of intrusive imagery. But the situation is probably not quite as straightforward as that since exposure can lead to habituation to the stimuli as well as oversensitivity to the stimuli.

Alexander and Wells (1991) studied a group of police officers who had been involved in retrieving and dealing with a large number of bodies which had been entombed in a submerged accommodation module for several months following an explosion on an oil platform. One unusual feature of this study was that it was possible to obtain a matched control group of officers, and also some of the officers involved in the retrieval duties had previously completed various psychological measures as part of an occupational health project. The data for sickness absence in the 12 months after the retrieval exercise were also examined.

No officer sought formal counselling or sought help from the Force Medical Officer following the recovery exercise. No significant differences were found in levels of anxiety and depression between officers who had previous experience of body handling and those who had no such experience. There was no evidence that the body handling in this incident had any impact on level of anxiety or depression: there was no difference in scores "before" and "after" and there was no difference between the control group and the body handling group in their symptom scores. Similarly there was no significant difference between the handling group and the control group in terms of the number of days off in the 12 months following the exercise. It is worth noting, however, that there were several unique aspects of this study: (i) officers were selected from departments where they were routinely exposed to deaths; (ii) less experienced officers were paired with more experienced officers; (iii) officers were given the opportunity to withdraw from these duties; (iv) debriefings were carried out each evening by senior police officers; (v) professional help was available, although not used by the officers; (vi) time had been available before the exercise to plan the whole thing and to prepare officers and to provide them with an intensive induction.

The recovery and identification of bodies and human remains is a task that the police undertake following any multiple fatality event. A number of reports have described the effect of such activities upon the recovery personnel. One of the most extensive studies in this area was conducted by Jones (1985) who surveyed 592 US Air Force personnel who had been responsible for the transportation and identification of almost 1000 bodies following a mass suicide in Jonestown, Guyana, in 1978. The Air Force personnel completed a self-report measure of the emotional effects of their experiences some 8 months after the event. Demographic details were also obtained and an estimate of the degree and duration of exposure that the individual officers had to the bodies was made. They were also questioned about any prior experience with human bodies or living accident victims. A control group of Air Force personnel, matched by rank and duties, who did not participate in the recovery task was also recruited. The final samples comprised 206 recovery personnel and 68 control respondents. These were all men; the very few women who had taken part were eliminated from the sample.

Jones (1985) found that the Guyana experience seemed to have had a short-term dysphoric effect on nearly one-third of the respondents but there did not seem to be a great rate of dysphoria among this sample when compared to the control group in the long term (ie after 8 months). Risk factors for short-term dysphoria were found to be: being less than 25 years of age; being black; being an enlisted respondent compared to an officer; and having a relatively greater degree of exposure to remains. Having previous training or experience in dealing with human remains was not found to be significantly related to risk of short-term dysphoria. However, among those who worked with remains over a protracted period, prior training and experience were protective.

Some of the problems with this study were that the self-assessment of emotional impact was made sometime after the event and that standardised assessments were not used. However, there is little other information available about the impact of such experiences and so this study does provide information about a relatively poorly understood area. The fact that black personnel were more affected was suggested to be linked to the fact that the victims themselves were predominantly black. Many respondents also reported that the impact of handling the bodies of infants and children was the greatest. Jones (1985) made a number of recommendations for dealing with the task of disaster victim recovery operations. These are given in Table 10.

Table 10. Recommended actions for dealing with disaster victim recovery operations

1. Older, experienced individuals should be used where possible or young people paired with older people

2. Day-to-day emotional support should be provided

3. Non-threatening group discussion should be facilitated to allow individuals to understand that others are experiencing similar strong emotions to them

4. There should be a normal termination for the group, who are given recognition by the appropriate and valued authorities

5. Debriefings should be provided

6. Follow-up mental health care should be made available

Source: adapted from D. R. Jones (1985). Secondary disaster victims: The emotional effects of recovering and identifying human remains. *American Journal of Psychiatry*, **142**, 303–307. Reproduced by permission of the American Psychiatric Association.

Butcher and Dunn (1989) have enumerated the kinds of difficulties that rescue workers face when dealing with the aftermath of airline disasters. These are given in Table 11.

Table 11. Difficulties faced by rescue workers following airline disasters

1. Stress arising from making critical decisions

2. Confrontation with human carnage

3. Mass destruction of property and environment

4. Distraught relatives and survivors

5. Pressure from their own families to return home

6. Interference from the media and onlookers

7. Dealing with situations for which they are not trained or prepared

8. Doubts about their decisions and ability to handle the job

9. Scapegoating by victims as a convenient focus for their anger

Source: adapted from J. N. Butcher and L. A. Dunn (1989). Human responses and treatment needs in airline disasters. In R. Gist and B. Lubin (Eds), *Psychosocial Aspects of Disaster*. New York: Wiley.

Raphael, Singh, Bradbury et al (1983–84) surveyed personnel who had been involved in rescue work following a rail disaster. They found that around a quarter of those in their sample experienced anxiety, depression and insomnia in the subsequent months. In a similar study, Berah, Jones and Valant (1984) studied the effect of a bushfire disaster on a volunteer mental health team. Most of the team reported some psychological or physical impact including feelings of shock, confusion, tiredness and changes in smoking, drinking and eating habits.

Risk Factors for Psychological Problems

The best predictor of long-term psychological response to a trauma is probably the initial impact on the person. McFarlane (1989) studied a group of 469 fire fighters at 4, 11 and 29 months after having been exposed to a bushfire disaster in Australia. He looked at the relative contributions of degree of exposure to the disaster, personal losses sustained, personality and past history of psychological disorder, to psychological state at the final assessment. While the severity of exposure to the disaster and the degree of personal loss sustained were related to psychological symptoms at 4 months, they were not related to psychological adjustment at 29 months.

PTSD can occur following a very wide variety of traumas, eg war, rape, natural disasters. The reasons why only some people experience PTSD following trauma are not clear. There have been a number of different theories about the underlying causes of PTSD, which have been reviewed by Jones and Barlow (1990).

PTSD can co-occur with other psychological problems, the most common of these being anxiety, depression and substance abuse. Suicidal thoughts are not uncommon. The onset of PTSD following a traumatic event is not always immediate. If the onset of symptoms is at least 6 months after the traumatic event then a diagnosis of "delayed" PTSD is given. Delayed PTSD may be triggered by exposure to a similar type of incident, by having to give evidence about the event at a court hearing or by exposure to some unrelated stressor.

It is not altogether clear why some individuals develop PTSD after exposure to a traumatic event and yet others do not. Some evidence suggests that individuals with a pre-existing history of psychological problems may be more at risk of psychological problems following a traumatic incident (eg Ruch, Chandler and Harter 1980) although few studies have examined PTSD risk factors as such. There are some indications that a family history of psychological problems may be associated with risk of PTSD (eg McFarlane 1989), but the role of personality and other vulnerability factors is less clear cut (McFarlane 1990).

Large-scale studies in the United States have found a rate of PTSD in the adult population of 1–2% (Helzer, Robins and McEvoy 1987). There are no definitive studies of the prevalence of PTSD among police officers but it has been suggested that around 12–35% of police officers suffer from PTSD (Boyle 1987; Mann and Neece 1990). Mann and Neece (1990) have reviewed the situation in the United States with respect to compensation through the courts for police officers' work-related PTSD. It is worth keeping in mind that PTSD is not the only kind of disorder that can result from exposure to severe or traumatic stressors. Depression, anxiety and abuse of alcohol or other substances are also common reactions. These are discussed in the following chapter.

In the study by Martin, McKean and Veltkamp (1986) referred to earlier in this chapter, police officers were asked to complete a checklist derived from DSM-III criteria for Post Traumatic Stress Disorder. The most frequently endorsed symptom (47%) was "recurrent and intrusive recollections of the event". Symptoms of PTSD were significantly more likely to have occurred in response to the trauma of having one's family threatened than other types of events. The conclusions that can be drawn from this study are limited by the small and unrepresentative sample but it is one of the few attempts to examine directly PTSD among police officers.

Claims through the courts for stress-related injuries and for PTSD in police officers who have been involved in traumatic incidents have been successful in the majority of States in the United States (Mann and Neece 1990). There have now also been several such cases in the British courts. If the number of such legal claims continues to increase then police forces will have to treat seriously the risk of PTSD following traumatic incidents. This has led to some forces having procedures in place for providing psychological help after such events.

Interventions Following Traumatic Incidents

The responses of different organisations to the needs of their staff following traumatic incidents will vary widely. However, there are a number of papers which describe the various types of strategies that might be used. For example, Hillenberg and Wolf (1988) have reviewed the role that Employee Assistance Programmes can play.

Suggestions for helping officers following exposure to traumatic incidents have come from a number of sources. Dunning and Silva (1980), as well as a number of other authors, have recommended the use of stress debriefing sessions. The aim of such sessions is to alert officers to potential signs of stress and to try to prevent any long-term psychological problems. Debriefing sessions are therefore proposed to have a number of elements: mutual support; education; emotional expression and release; and demonstration of institutional acceptance of the reactions of those involved.

"Critical Incident Stress Debriefing Teams" have been suggested by Mitchell (1983) as a way of offering help to emergency services personnel following a traumatic incident, and in preparing such personnel for job-related stress. Details of such debriefings are outlined in Chapter 6. Dealing with reactions to disasters falls into three broad categories: education, support and crisis intervention (Wilkinson and Vera 1989). Education of police officers could obviously form part of their routine training. They should be made aware of what kind of psychological and physiological symptoms are to be expected following exposure to extreme situations, how to cope with these symptoms and how to obtain professional help if they need it. This basic information should also be provided at debriefing sessions for officers and other involved staff immediately following any major event. General support is best provided by a peer group of officers who have shared in the experience being given time to share their reactions with one another. Crisis intervention is best supplied by a professional mental health worker whose aim would be to restore the individual, whose coping resources are swamped, to their usual level of functioning as quickly as possible. The supposed advantages of early intervention have not been fully evaluated, however Duckworth (1991b) has suggested what such advantages might be. In the first place any psychological problems will be less entrenched and therefore treatment should be easier and quicker. Also the person's resources should still be relatively intact and they may be both more able and more motivated to cooperate with any treatment. Early intervention may therefore prevent the development of more serious difficulties.

The role of family support is less clear cut. Many officers do not talk about the nature of their duties or their emotional reactions to the family members. This is sometimes because the officers do not expect their families to be able to understand the situation or, more usually, because they wish to avoid distressing the family by vicariously exposing them to the trauma.

In some cases in the United Kingdom, local government has taken it upon itself to resource the necessary counselling or support services subsequent to a disaster. For example, following the Bradford City Football Club fire, the local city council targeted the services of their social services department both at the survivors of the disaster and at the emergency services personnel (Bradford City Council 1985). In commenting on the general contribution that social services have to make in the aftermath of a disaster, Brook (1990) has sounded a note of caution:

> the nature and scale of services provided by social workers, however, is guided by a "received knowledge" which has evolved over the last four years without the benefit of serious criticism or evaluation, or of a sound understanding of the implications of relevant research.

A large number of pieces have been published that deal with the mental health aspects of disasters, eg Ahearn (1985), Raphael (1986), and Clegg (1988).

Treatment of PTSD

A variety of different approaches to the treatment of PTSD have been tried (eg Horowitz 1976; Kolb 1986) but there is no consensus about the most effective single type of treatment. In the initial stages of PTSD some kind of crisis intervention will usually be called for. The advantage of early and active intervention is that while the individual's psychological defences are weakened it is possible to make therapeutic progress relatively quickly. Duckworth (1991a) reports that at the Hillsborough football stadium crush disaster a professional psychologist and a welfare officer were called to the scene within two hours to provide psychological debriefings and "first aid". They then produced an information sheet within 24 hours which described the kinds of reactions that people might expect to have, the counselling support available and the kind of problems that might require professional help.

Scurfield (1985) has described five treatment principles for interventions with PTSD to address long-term effects. These are listed in Table 12.

Table 12. Treatment principles for Post Traumatic Stress Disorder

1.	Establishment of the therapeutic trust relationship
2.	Education regarding the stress recovery process
3.	Stress management/reduction
4.	Regression back to or a re-experiencing of the trauma
5.	Integration of the trauma experience

Source: adapted from R. M. Scurfield (1985). Post-trauma stress assessment and treatment: Overview and formulations. In C. R. Figley (Ed.), *Trauma and its Wake*. New York: Brunner/Mazel.

Prevention

Those authors who have addressed the issue of the prevention of PTSD have tended to concentrate on an early intervention in the immediate aftermath of a traumatic incident as being potentially useful in limiting its development. However, there has been little in the way of systematic evaluation of such efforts to establish if in fact early intervention is effective in preventing the full syndrome of PTSD from occurring. Most studies that have been published have tended to be descriptive accounts such as that by Brom and

Kebler (1989) describing a preventive programme in the Netherlands.

There may be a role for pre-trauma training or preparation to be built into routine police training (Frederick 1978). This could include some rehearsal of the cognitive and affective responses that might be expected, and an overview of the kinds of coping responses that might be most effective in dealing with the situation. The New Zealand police force have a training module on "Trauma" in which post-traumatic reactions are described and information given about the available support services. Miller (1992) has described a specific training to help officers who might be involved in Disaster Victim Identification work. He suggests that such pre-incident training can provide officers with an opportunity to examine their likely psychological responses in a relatively non-threatening way. Miller has used a progressive exposure training programme which involves the use of videos and photographs initially, then a realistic exercise using dead animals, followed by visiting the mortuary and attending a post mortem. However, the feasibility and usefulness of such training need to be explored further.

There may also be a role in initial selection and training of police officers. For example, in the Phillips and Cochrane (1991) study of assaults on the police it was suggested that officers who used more confrontational policing methods might be more at risk of assault. These authors therefore suggested that more emphasis be given in training on the use of non-confrontational techniques. In addition, the "at risk" individuals might be identified at an early stage, either at the point of selection or when in the job. Remedial training could then be offered to such individuals. Davies (1988) describes "violence prevention" workshops which train professional carers in techniques to help them avoid physical attack by their clients. Such training can equip an employee to be more competent in a range of circumstances, to improve their interpersonal skills and to help staff to recognise and diffuse aggression at an early stage (Poyner and Warne 1986). Some police forces have introduced protective screens in their front offices, especially when employing civilians as station duty officers. This is in line with other organisations whose members of staff come into contact with the public and where there is the possibility of threats or assaults (Poyner and Warne 1986).

SUMMARY

Neither exposure to traumatic incidents nor the possibility of suffering Post Traumatic Stress Disorder is unique to the police. Incidents which are likely to involve police officers include criminal violence, disasters or accidents, and public disorder. There is little of substance available that provides insight into the experience and consequences for police officers in their involvement in public order policing. Involvement in assaults, being shot at, shooting at others, and rescue work at natural or technological disasters have been associated with symptoms of Post Traumatic Stress Disorder. Symptoms of this disorder have been listed within the diagnostic manuals of the American Psychiatric Association and include: persistent and intrusive memories of the traumatic incident, avoidance of feelings associated with the event, loss of interest and feeling as well as difficulties in sleeping and concentrating. Clinicians, however, have experienced a number of difficulties in diagnosing Post Traumatic Stress Disorder as often sufferers themselves do not reveal the traumatic incident. In addition there may be some secondary symptoms such as excessive drinking which mask the traumatic stress. The imagery associated with the trauma can be mistaken as being indicative of other conditions. Two tragedies in particular have been the subject of research that has yielded insight into the impact of such events on those sent to assist. The Piper Alpha oil platform disaster and the mass suicide of a religious cult membership in Jonestown, Guyana, offered opportunities to study the effects of mass body handling on emergency workers. It would seem that prior training can have a protective inoculation effect to insulate some workers from Post Traumatic Stress Disorder. Debriefing sessions after exposure have also been used to assist officers to deal with feelings aroused by their involvement in rescue work. However, there is no consensus about the most effective single type of treatment. Moreover, the reasons why only some individuals experience Post Traumatic Stress Disorder is not entirely clear. A family or individual history of psychological problems has been implicated as a risk factor.

CHAPTER 4

Stress Casualties

There are a number of ways in which stress might produce adverse effects in the individual. There are three main types of adverse effects:

(i)   impaired job performance;
(ii)   psychological problems;
(iii)   physical health problems.

In this chapter each of these types of effects will be examined in turn. The factors that make some people more vulnerable to stress and its effects than others will also be examined. Both physical and psychological stress-related disorders were found to occur more frequently in police officers than in other occupational groups in a study of 130 occupations conducted by Fell, Richard and Wallace (1980).

IMPAIRED JOB PERFORMANCE

Impaired job performance includes difficulties in carrying out duties effectively and efficiently as well as absenteeism and pre-mature retirement. Some of the first signs of stress in the individual that might be noticed in the workplace are difficulties in concentrating, increased forgetfulness, turning up late for work, loss of interest and motivation, or lengthening of lunch breaks.

Sickness absence obviously reduces the efficiency of the police service. In 1985, it was estimated that each year in England and Wales the police service lost 1.6 million working days through sickness: nearly 13.5 days per officer per year (Sharrock 1988). British Home Office figures for 1987 revealed that the number of days taken as sick leave throughout police forces in England and Wales was equivalent to the loss of 5000 officers. Moreover, between 1980 and 1985 the national average number of days lost per officer rose from 12 in 1980 to 14 in 1985. One British police force calculated that its staffing level was effectively reduced by 300 through sickness absence and that the cost to it was over £3 million per year (Woolfenden 1989).

There has been relatively little research into the causes and contexts of sickness absence in police forces. Consequently, direct empirical evidence that stress is a significant contributory factor in sickness absence is scarce.

PSYCHOLOGICAL PROBLEMS

Psychiatric Disorders

The most common psychological problems in the general population are depression, anxiety and alcohol problems. Relatively little is known about the relationship, if any, between occupation and risk of neurotic disorders such as anxiety and depression. One of the few studies in this area is that conducted by Eaton, Anthony, Mandel and Garrison (1990). They examined rates of depression among more than 100 different occupations and occupational groupings in the USA. The two occupations with the highest prevalence of major depressive disorder were data entry keyers and computer equipment operators. Unfortunately police officers were not examined as a discrete occupational group in terms of overall prevalence. When the data were reanalysed controlling for gender, education, ethnicity and current employment status, those occupational groups most likely to be depressed were lawyers, non-college teachers and secretaries. However, this study did not address the issue of why some occupational groups are more at risk than others.

Alcohol and Drug Misuse

Alcohol problems have been thought to be particularly prevalent among police officers. Plant (1981) has listed eight risk factors associated with occupations which have high rates of alcoholism. These are given in Table 13.

Table 13.   Risk factors related to alcoholism and occupations

1. Availability of alcohol

2. Social pressure to drink

3. Separation from family due to work commitments

4. Lack of supervision

5. High or low income levels

6. Collusion in excessive drinking by colleagues

7. Strains and stresses

8. Recruitment of those predisposed to drink heavily

Source: adapted from M. A. Plant (1981). Risk factors in employment. In B. D. Hore and M. A. Plant (Eds), *Alcohol Problems in Employment*. London: Croom Helm.

Around one-quarter of US police officers have been claimed to have a significant problem with alcohol (Kroes 1976). An Australian survey has reported higher rates of alcohol consumption amongst detectives compared to a control group (Cacioppe and Mock 1985) but that report also noted that there is little official evidence available on drinking rates in Australian police forces.

Brown, Cooper and Dudman (1992), in their study of senior police officers in the British police service, found that such officers claim to drink significantly less than the general population, with 25% claiming either to be non-drinkers or only to drink on social occasions. This compares to 17% of non- or social drinkers in the general population.

Clearly alcohol or other drugs may be used to ameliorate anxiety or depression or other distress. However, use only becomes abuse if certain features are present: (i) if the individual cannot stop or cut down their use; (ii) work, family or social life is negatively affected; and, (iii) the substance abuse problem has lasted for at least one month.

In the US, it is estimated that at least 10% of adults have some kind of social, psychological or medical problem arising from alcohol use and of that 10% about half are thought to be addicted to alcohol (Rosenhan and Seligman 1984). In their study of a British police force, Alexander, Innes, Irving, Sinclair and Walker (1991) found that 15% of male and female officers reported levels of alcohol consumption which would be designated as "moderate" or "high" risk by the standards set by the British Royal Colleges of Psychiatrists and Physicians. However, they report that this proportion was not statistically different from the proportion falling into the same categories among fire officers, prison officers or nurses. There were also differences by rank and duties: moderate/high risk drinking was more common in male constables than in higher ranks.

Suicide

Male police officers in the United Kingdom have lower suicide rates than men in other occupational groups (Office of Population Census and Surveys 1988). They have less than half the rate of judges, barristers or solicitors and are a quarter of the rate among dental practitioners. However, in the United States, elevated suicide rates among police officers have been reported by a number of authors (eg Violanti, Vena and Marshall 1986; Gularnick 1963). Fell, Richard and Wallace (1980) found that police officers in the United States had the third highest suicide rate among 130 occupations. Rates of suicide amongst Australian police officers would appear to be relatively low. Cacioppe and Mock (1985) provide some evidence from the New South Wales Police indicating suicide rates to be significantly lower than in the general population.

White (1982) examined the suicide rates among the Royal Ulster Constabulary in Northern Ireland. He found that the rate was 14.5 per 100 000 for the period 1922–1969. From 1970–1982 the rate was 8.5 per 100 000. Both of these rates were higher than that for the general population from which they were drawn (4.3 per 100 000). The Royal Ulster Constabulary also has "reserve" members and their suicide rates were very high in comparison at 21.9 per 100 000 (for part timers) and 16.8 per 100 000 (for full timers). However, it must be noted that since its inception in 1922, the Royal Ulster Constabulary has had to carry out both normal policing functions and functions associated with the armed struggle that has become an intrinsic part of the scene in Northern Ireland. Unlike their police colleagues in mainland Britain, RUC officers are routinely issued with firearms and therefore have a readily available means of suicide.

Marital Problems

There has been a common assumption made that police officers have higher divorce rates than other groups in the community. Terry (1981) reviewed some of the evidence for the higher divorce rates among police officers and concluded that police divorce rates in the United States were lower than the national average. However, he does caution that many of the studies carried out in this area suffer from problems of design or method that limit their generalisability. In particular Terry (1981) notes that most studies of police divorce rate have failed to distinguish between police officers who were divorced before they joined the police and those who were divorced subsequent to joining the police.

The question of whether or not aspects of being a police officer have a negative impact on marital relationships is even more difficult to address than the issue of divorce rates. Studies have tended to assert that any marital problems observed in police officers' families can be attributed to features of the job, the most common of these being shiftwork and unpredictability of hours. The majority of studies in this area have, of course, focused on the male police officer and there is little, if any, empirical data about the effect of the job on policewomen's relationships.

PHYSICAL HEALTH PROBLEMS

The physical health problems that can arise from stressors in life cover a wide variety of different types. They include hypertension (high blood pressure); heart problems; stomach ulcers; respiratory problems; and skin problems. In some of these there is a direct physiological link between being subjected to various stressors and subsequent physical disorders. For example, when under pressure an individual's heart rate will increase and blood pressure will rise. However, it can be difficult to demonstrate unequivocally that such immediate changes can themselves lead to ongoing high blood pressure.

Other effects of stress on physical health status are more indirect and are brought about via the changes in behaviour or lifestyle that are the consequence of exposure to stressors. Examples of this would be behaviours such as smoking or drinking which themselves can be triggered or exacerbated by stress and then have an adverse effect on physical health.

It should not be overlooked that physical ill-health can itself be an important stressor for the individual. Acute illness episodes may well give rise to anxiety and depressive disorders. Especially in organisations such as the police force, individuals may worry particularly about the effect of physical ill-health upon their ability to continue in their job. Chronic ill-health may be minimised or hidden in order to avoid the possible threat of loss of employment. Physical injury while at work can give rise to psychological problems. In a study of 107 accidentally injured adults, Malt (1988) found that almost 17% had had a subsequent psychiatric disorder.

Illnesses that are thought to be particularly associated with stress are sometimes called "psychosomatic" or "psychophysiological" disorders. For example, it is known that high rates of peptic ulcers have been found in people in occupations that might be thought of as stressful. Cobb and Rose (1973) found that air traffic controllers had twice the rate of a control group and that the amount of air traffic that controllers had to deal with was related to their risk of ulcers.

Violanti, Vena and Marshall (1986) followed up a sample of 2376 police officers from New York State. They also had comparative data on morbidity and mortality among a municipal worker sample and the general population. Overall the mortality rate from all causes was much the same for police officers as for the US white male general population. When compared with municipal workers, the police officers were found to have almost three times the suicide rate. Higher risks were also found among police officers, compared to municipal workers, for cancers of the oesophagus and the colon, and for ulcers. There was a complex picture found for heart disease: for officers employed in the police service for 10–19 years there was a significantly lower than expected mortality but for those employed for more than 40 years there was a significantly increased risk. Violanti, Vena and Marshall (1986) suggest that the elevated rates of cancers of the digestive organs may be attributable to the police occupational lifestyle of shiftwork, irregular and poor eating habits, smoking, and alcohol and caffeine intake. In an earlier study in Washington State, Milham (1983) reported that police have an increased risk of mortality from cancers of the colon and liver, diabetes and heart disease. Similarly Gularnick (1963) found police officers to be more likely to suffer from heart disease and diabetes and to be more likely to commit suicide.

In a study of British police officers, Brown and Forde (1989) were able to compare reported physical health status by rank (Table 14). Within ranks, probationer constables were the least likely to report any physical health problems.

Mortality

Data available in the United Kingdom from the Office of Population Censuses and Surveys (Office of Population Census and Surveys 1988) on occupational mortality provide interesting comparisons among police officers of different ranks. Table 15 gives the Standardised Mortality Ratios (SMR) for police officers by rank and gender. The Standardised Mortality Ratio is based on a method of calculation where a figure of 100 is taken to be the "average" mortality ratio. Thus a figure greater than 100 represents an elevated mortality rate compared to the average and a figure below 100 a less than average rate.

The figures that stand out in this table are the higher than average mortality rates for sergeants of both sexes. However, it must be noted that these figures are a rather crude index and they do not allow for other factors which might be associated with rank (eg smoking or other lifestyle factors) and may confound any association between rank and mortality rates.

Table 14. Physical health of British police officers by rank

	Probationer constables (%)	Police constables (%)	Sergeants (%)	Inspectors (%)	Chief Inspectors (%)	General[a] male population (%)
During the last 2 weeks did you have to cut down on any of the things you usually do because of illness or injury?	6	18	15	8	7	11
During the last 3 months did you attend as an outpatient or casualty at a hospital emergency or outpatient clinic?	11	19	12	13	15	13
During the past 3 months have you been in hospital as an inpatient?	4	4	5	4	0	8
Do you have any long standing illness or disability or infirmity? By long standing I mean anything medical, physical or mental that has troubled you over a long period of time	9	23	22	22	19	31

Source: Brown and Forde (1989) and [a]OPCS (1989).

Table 15. Standardised mortality ratios (SMR) for British police officers by gender and rank

	SMR 1979–80
Male senior officers	102
Female senior officers	47
Male sergeants	159
Female sergeants	135
Males below sergeants	94
Females below sergeants	44

Source: OPCS (1988).

It is also possible, using the OPCS data (Office of Population Census and Surveys 1988) to examine interprofessional death rates. In Table 16 the mean annual death rates per 100 000 of the population for men aged 20–64 are given. In this table age has been taken into account. The fact that male sergeants are found to have a mean annual death rate that is around twice that of other police officers is very striking. It should also be noted that other ranks of police officers have elevated death rates compared to other emergency service and prison service personnel.

Table 16. Mean annual death rates by occupational group

	Mean annual death rates
Police inspectors and above	743
Sergeants	1517
Officers below sergeants	787
Chief prison officers and above	648
Other prison officers	560
Fire service officers	528
Firemen	553
Traffic wardens	609

Source: OPCS (1988).

Although age is controlled for in these figures, it is still necessary to treat them with some caution since it is not known whether there are sociodemographic, socioenvironmental or behavioural differences between these occupational groups that might be responsible for the observed differential rates rather than aspects of their occupational role per se.

FACTORS WHICH MAKE SOME PEOPLE MORE VULNERABLE

Many different factors have been examined by researchers to see whether they have any role to play in determining who suffers adverse consequences after exposure to stress and who manages to escape without any such adverse consequences. Those factors which have been examined more carefully include: age; ethnicity; gender; occupation; personality factors; occupational characteristics such as rank, specialism and availability of social support. The remaining part of this chapter explores these in general terms and assesses the available empirical evidence. A fuller elaboration of the experiences of special groups working within the policing environment is given in the following chapter.

Intraindividual Factors

Considerable work has been undertaken on individual personality differences associated with stress-related symptoms. The objective has been to establish if certain personality types are more predisposed to suffer adversely following exposure to stressors. Thus, research findings suggest that an extrovert personality type, which is associated with stimulation seeking, tends to remain stable under pressure and report fewer unpleasant feelings than introverts in anticipatory situations (Davidson and Veno 1980). These authors also review work indicating association between neuroticism and adverse reactions. Research attempting to identify a "police personality" has been considerable and varied. The difficulties of establishing reliable and generalisable data have been reviewed by Lefkowitz (1975) who suggests that much previous literature relies on "informed opinions of persons experienced in the law enforcement field but [which are] subjective, often unsystematic and largely unverifiable". The conclusion by Lefkowitz is that whilst some evidence may support some recurring features in police officers' personality characteristics, there are virtually no data to support a conclusion that these are pathological.

In Davidson's survey of Australian police officers (Davidson 1979), measurement on the Eysenck Personality Inventory (EPI) indicated that the officers from Northern Territories were no more extroverted or introverted than the general population, although their neuroticism scores were higher than normative scores. Gudjonsson and Adlam (1983) measured personality characteristics of four different groups of British police officers: 84 recruits, 84 probationary constables, 73 experienced constables and 112 officers of senior rank. They found that neuroticism scores were normally distributed for their police officer samples and they did not differ significantly from normative scores.

Studies attempting to find other police personality characteristics such as conservatism, dogmatism and authoritarianism face difficulties in that their samples are often small and located in one particular police force, which makes generalising results difficult. It is also not unreasonable to suppose that recruitment policies and occupational socialisation play a role in selecting and shaping a police officer's "working personality" (Coleman and Gorman 1982). But as Davidson and Veno (1980) point out, there is no reason to assume that such characteristics, whilst not necessarily being socially desirable, will always exert adverse consequences when exposed to occupational stress. Also, Brown and Willis (1985) suggest that the informal working styles of more experienced officers encourage authoritarian behaviour amongst the younger officers that they tutor.

Beutler, Nussbaum and Meredith (1988) conducted a four-year follow-up study of 25 police recruits using the Minnesota Multiphasic Personality Inventory (MMPI). They report results which supported their hypothesis that the police service itself is associated with adverse psychological changes amongst officers. The 11 officers in the follow-up phase of the study, whilst representing a small number for reliable and valid comparisons, did show evidence of being at greater risk for stress-related physical complaints and substance abuse. However, these authors themselves cautioned against "unbridled generalization" from such a small sample and also indicated that the mean scores indicating this risk remained within the range of normal functioning. Also no external corroboration was available from others on their drinking or potential substance abuse.

Chandler and Jones (1979) discuss the notion of the cynical personality type and suggest that the adverse exposure to stressors can result in a cluster of reactions typified by overseriousness, emotional withdrawal, coldness, authoritarian attitudes and cynicism. They conclude, however, that there are many elements in police work that may push an individual towards adoption of cynical attitudes or actions but that the "cynical cop" as a concept is statistically invalid and unreliable.

The other major body of work investigating individual stress differences has been the examination of behaviour patterns associated with coronary heart disease (CHD) (Cooper and Marshall 1976). Type "A" behaviour pattern has been the term given to describe a particular style associated with an increased risk of CHD. It is characterised by high self-demand for achievement, and associated with competitiveness, striving and a tendency to suppress fatigue in order to meet deadlines. Such a life style is positively related to the likelihood of suffering CHD. Type "B" individuals are characterised by an absence of type A behaviours and have significantly lower incidences of CHD.

The presence of more police officers with type A personalities than in the general population has been established through research studies (Kirmeyer and Diamond 1985). Davidson and Veno (1980) report that up to 75% of Australian and American police samples in a number of studies have type A behaviour patterns. Robinson (1981) found a higher rate of type A responses amongst his British police sample than in the general population.

The question posed by Davidson and Veno (1980) is pertinent here: do the police attract type A persons into the service or does the organisation promote type A behaviour? This clearly relates to possible interventions to mitigate potential adverse health consequences. There is some suggestive, but inconclusive, evidence that both things might be happening.

Interorganisational Factors

Within the police service, there are a range of organisational and structural features which have been postulated to relate to greater or lesser stressfulness. Thus geographic location, rank and role of police staff have been thought to influence susceptibility to adverse reactions. Whilst there is considerable research purporting to show that urban-based police suffer more distress than rural police officers, the evidence from a variety of studies on the healthiness of rural and urban populations is inconsistent. What studies of the police tend to show is that there are different sources of stress acting upon rural and urban officers. Davidson and Veno (1980) report that rural officers are more likely to be affected by transfer policies, delays whilst on duty and lack of social privacy. Urban officers are more likely to suffer longer working hours and more irregularity in shift work. Cooper and Grimley (1983) found in their study of detectives in one British police force that those based in urban locations seem to suffer more adverse consequences associated with their dealings with offenders, major incidents such as murder, taking and executing warrants and coping with the press.

Data from Brown and Forde (1989) suggest that rural officers are significantly less likely to report feeling stressed by specific operational stressors or by organisational stressors. This is shown in Table 17.

Cain (1973) found differences between British rural and city police officers in terms of their social isolation. Rural officers tend to hold themselves aloof from the community in order to avoid potentially difficult conflict situations where they might have to exert authority. City police officers tended to experience isolation from their community as a consequence of the community imposing it on them rather than their choosing it voluntarily. The geographic location of officers is likely to have an impact on the type of work they do and hence indirectly affect their risk of suffering from adverse consequences of stress.

Table 17. Mean felt stress scores by location of officers
and type of stressors

	Police Operational stressors[a]	Organisational stressors[b]
City	7.8	23.3
Town	7.3	23.1
Conurbation	6.3	21.8
Rural	5.9	18.0
Island	7.1	20.2

[a]Total possible score 52; [b]Total possible score 164
Source: Brown and Forde (1989).

Officers engaged in different types of duties are thought to have
different patterns of exposure to stressors and vary in their adverse reactions. Cooper and Grimley (1983) studied sources of
stress amongst police detectives in one large British police force.
The study used the Middlesex Hospital Questionnaire as a measure of psychological distress and a type A behaviour questionnaire. Three factors were found to predict overall psychological
symptoms amongst the detectives: poor organisational management; stress-prone personality predisposition; and work factors
impinging on home life. However, the contribution of these factors
to psychological symptoms, whilst statistically significant, was
actually very small. These factors have also been found to be
associated with adverse stress reactions amongst officers on general patrol duties (Brown and Campbell 1990). Cooper and Grimley
suggest that there is a greater propensity for type A personalities
to be present in the Criminal Investigation Department (CID).
They propose that the process of investigation requires an
aggressive, time-conscious, hard-driving type of individual.
However, it is unclear whether such individuals self-select into
the CID or whether the working practices of the department
encourage this pattern of behaviour. Robinson (1981) showed
from his analysis of another British force that detectives experience
a greater frustration with inflexible decision-making than other

departments, ie traffic, uniformed patrol or administration. More-over detectives also appear to suffer more from having a sense of competition with other departments than officers from those departments. Officers from the CID are also more stressed by judicial criticism of police action or case presentation than others.

Police controllers and dispatchers are those who are involved in receipt of requests for police assistance and the assigning of units to deal with the incidents. The processing of insufficient informa-tion and time pressures were particular sources of stress identified by Sewell and Crew (1984) in a study carried out in the United States. They point out that many police dispatchers are not sworn police personnel, a trend that is paralleled in the British police service. It is the fact of their being civilian that Sewell and Crew (1984) identify as adding to their occupational stressors since they are limited in terms of their police knowledge and flexibility of discretion. However, Chadwick et al (1989) and Funnelle, Brown and Woolfenden (1991) found few differences between the stress levels of police and civilian despatchers in their studies in two British police forces. Where dispatchers, whether police or civilian personnel, differ from their police operational colleagues is in the physical confinement of their work location. The dispatcher is tied to the communication console which Sewell and Crew (1984) found to be a particular source of stress.

Ely and Mostardi (1986) examined a series of physiological mea-sures associated with adverse stress reactions amongst uniformed officers, detectives, service officers and traffic officers in Akron City Police Department. The actual duties of the service officers were not made clear. Comparing all police officer respondents with controls—a group of clerical staff working in other city departments—the former had higher norepinephrine levels and higher diastolic blood pressure. When comparing officers by types of duties, there were no differences on any of the measures between uniformed, detective or traffic officers. There were differ-ences between uniformed and service officers with the latter having higher rates. Brown and Forde (1989) examined level of stress by type of duties that officers were assigned to. Table 18 illustrates the differences between various types of officers.

Table 18. Proportions of various types of officers reporting felt stress from various stressors

	Custody/ Supervisory duties (%)	CID (%)	Car drivers (%)	Uniform foot patrol (%)
Organisational and management stressors				
Dirty, noisy, drab environment	91	97	88	90
Work overload	64	61	70	75
Time pressures	64	74	79	77
Lack of consultation	91	90	95	88
Lack of support from senior officers	94	92	91	90
Staff shortages	83	81	86	80
Inadequate resources	89	90	86	92
Shifts	56	39	56	44
Long hours	59	43	63	58
Police operational stressors				
Searching for a missing person	8	12	9	12
Appearing in Crown Court	19	14	30	28
Arresting a violent person	67	61	68	75
Public order duties	68	70	75	63
Answering a call for assistance	33	48	37	42
Football duty	20	0	23	28
Dealing with sudden death	65	55	61	62
Minor injury on duty	72	77	80	85
Informing relative of sudden death	83	91	85	79
Dealing with victims of violence	56	58	52	49
Dealing with victims of sex offence	70	70	75	74

Source: Brown and Forde (1989).

Detectives were least likely to suffer adverse consequences from shift work or long hours and, overall, were less likely to be involved in a range of routine police duties from which they reported adverse effects.

Rank perhaps has been the most studied occupational variable felt to be associated with potential for adverse stress reactions. Cooper, Davidson and Robinson (1982) and Brown and Campbell (1990) showed that distinctive patterns of exposure to stressors were associated with rank of officer in the British policing context. Cooper, Davidson and Robinson (1982) looked at physical and psychological measures of distress and found different predictors for different ranks.

Brown and Campbell (1990) show quite clearly in their study that police operational stressors decreasingly impinge on higher ranked officers, whilst management-generated stressors operate in the opposite direction. This has the effect of placing the sergeant in the key position where the conduct of operational tasks and management tasks intersects, making this the rank where potentially the greatest number and variety of stressors impinge (Table 19 and Figure 1).

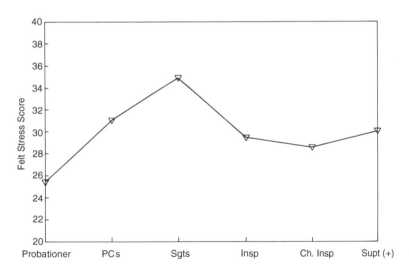

Figure 1. Total mean felt stress score (organisational and operational stressors) by rank of officer. Source: Brown and Ford (1989).

Table 19. Proportion of officers by rank admitting stress associated with organisational and management stressors

	Prob-ationer (%)	PC (%)	Sgt (%)	Insp (%)	Chief Insp (%)	Supt & higher ranks (%)
Staff manpower shortages	75	83	86	83	70	75
Lack of consultation	100	92	95	91	74	80
Time pressures	73	77	69.	62	59	57
Demands of work vs home	90	91	92	96	64	91
Inadequate resources	100	88	89	91	88	79
Lack of senior support	100	91	96	94	75	100
Shift work	43	54	53	57	0	0
Work overload	74	70	66	68	44	57
Drab surroundings	17	93	91	91	86	89
Very long hours	59	60	59	47	39	52

Source: Brown and Forde (1989).

Robinson (1981) found that the sergeants in his study of the Greater Manchester Police believed themselves to suffer job over-load and to be especially inhibited by bureaucratic obstacles that interfered with rather than facilitated their supervision and management. The officers at the next level, inspectors and chief inspectors, particularly suffered from autocratic management styles. Senior officers, superintendents and chief superintendents reported being stressed by volume of paperwork and problems associated with the courts and resolving conflicts between the police and community and with the press.

Brown, Cooper and Dudman (1992) examined stress amongst senior officers in the United Kingdom having the rank of superintendent or chief superintendent. The Occupational Stress Inventory (OSI) was used and additional occupational and demographic details were also obtained. Just over 800 questionnaires were sent to officers throughout the United Kingdom, yielding a 66% return. Overall, these officers were less likely to smoke and drink than the general population and were also less likely to have been a recent hospital patient than the population at large. The most frequently mentioned sources of stress were having too much work, staff shortages, insufficient finance and resources and lack of consultation and communication. Nine out of ten of these senior officers said that they coped with job stressors by planning ahead, dealing with problems immediately, setting priorities, having stable home relationships and trying to deal with situations objectively. Interestingly, sharing a home life with a partner who was also pursuing a career was least likely to be mentioned as a source of stress, so too was having to work with members of the opposite sex. The overwhelming majority of officers at this rank are men; there are just over 30 women officers who serve at this rank in the United Kingdom compared with nearly 2540 men. The study revealed no gender differences in levels of reported stress, or health outcomes. In an interesting comparison with 1556 senior managers from private industry, the superintendents were significantly less likely to report Type "A" behaviour patterns (Table 20). The private sector managers were more likely to indicate sources of stress that were intrinsic to the job, eg having too much work to do, keeping up with new techniques, career

Table 20. Comparisons between police managers and private industry managers on health indices

Health indices	Police	Private industry
Mental health	47.3	48.7
Physical health	27.3	27.4
Attitude of living	21.9	22.3
Style of behaviour	18.6	18.9
Ambition	11.1	11.9
Type "A" behaviour	51.6	53.1

Source: Brown, Cooper and Dudman (1992).

achievement-related stressors and home–work interface problems than police superintendents. However, police superintendents report greater stress associated with organisational structure or climate than their private sector counterparts.

Extra-organisational Comparisons

There are relatively few available studies that compare police officers with other occupational groups. In part, comparisons are problematic because of the nature of the populations. Thus police forces tend to be made up of predominantly male personnel, between the ages of 18 and 50 years. Officers are selected in for their physical fitness and screened out if they become ill or incapacitated. In addition, it is difficult to equate the type of work performed by different occupational groupings. Earlier in this chapter, divorce and suicide rates were mentioned in which it was unclear whether police officers suffered elevated rates when compared with the general population. Davidson (1979) reports higher rates of neuroticism amongst the Northern Territories police, whilst Ely and Mostardi (1986) found elevated physiological indicators of stress when comparing their American police and control samples.

Cacioppe and Mock (1985) reported results for an Australian sample of senior staff in a variety of public and private sector organisations. Senior police officers were not found to report stress symptoms at a greater rate than business managers who had amongst the lowest scores when compared with other public sector administrators. Brown and Campbell (1990) demonstrated that their British police officer samples were less likely than the general population to have physical health problems and fewer police officers were smokers than in the population at large. They also suggested that the sources of stress for police managers and those in nursing and teaching are a combination of their respective front line duties and management systems. The front line duties are less frequent in all three occupations than organisational problems. Poor management, inadequate staffing, insufficient resources, lack of communication and support are all nominated as sources of stress by police, nurses and teachers.

Brown, Cooper and Dudman (1992) found that their British police superintendent sample were less likely to smoke or drink than the general population (Table 21). When compared with private sector managers, the police superintendents were less likely to be subject to similar job stressors apart from those related to organisational climate and culture. Superintendents reported higher exposure to these than the commercial managers. This study found some evidence to suggest that police officers may be in better physical and psychological shape than the general population, but there are probable recruitment, selection and retirement policies to account, in part, for this. There is less evidence available to suggest that the police suffer more adversely from occupational stress than other groups, and some evidence that in fact they are exposed to fewer stressors and are less likely to suffer adverse reactions.

Table 21. Health of police superintendents compared with the general male population

	General male[a] population (%)	Police[b] Superintendents (%)
During the last 2 weeks did you have to cut down on any of the things you usually do because of illness or injury?	11	9
During the last 3 months did you attend as an outpatient or casualty at a hospital emergency or outpatient clinic?	13	11
During the past 3 months have you been in hospital as an inpatient for any complaint or operation?	8	1.5
Do you have any long standing illness or disability or infirmity? By long standing I mean anything medical, physical or mental that has troubled you over a long period of time	31	21
Non-smokers	67	80
Non or occasional drinkers	17	25

Sources: [a] OPCS (1989) and Central Statistical Office (1991); [b] Brown, Cooper and Dudman (1992).

SUMMARY

Adverse consequences arising from exposure to occupational stressors have been identified as impaired job performance, psychological problems and physical health disorders. Early warning signs include: difficulties in concentrating; forgetfulness; turning up late for work; loss of interest; and loss of motivation. Sickness absence is the most obvious effect impacting upon the organisation itself.

There is no clear cut evidence that psychiatric disorders occur amongst police officers at any different rate from those occurring in the general population either in Britain or other countries. Similarly the evidence is equivocal for any greater incidence of alcohol-related problems amongst police officers than others in society at large. There have been claims that suicide rates and the occurrence of marital breakdown amongst police officers are higher than in other groups in the population. Again the evidence is not strong enough to confirm this as a consistent finding.

With respect to physical health problems, then certain ranks of officer do seem to have relatively high rates of mortality or morbidity. Physical ill-health itself can be a personal stressor for an individual as well as a potential consequence following exposure to occupational stressors.

A number of factors have been proposed to be associated with a greater susceptibility to adverse reactions to occupational stressors. These include age, ethnicity, gender, personality as well as certain characteristics of the individual's occupational profile such as rank held and specialism occupied.

The evidence for personality correlates and stress resistance or proneness is inconclusive. Demographic features such as gender and ethnicity may be related to distinctive aspects of exposure to stressors rather than susceptibility to symptoms. Differential exposure has as much to do with the organisation's culture as with these characteristics per se. Indeed there is some evidence that police culture itself is associated with the encouragement of adverse psychological characteristics such as the development of authoritarianism.

Rank and specialism of officer have been found to be associated with distinctive patterns of exposure to sources of occupational stress as well as severity of self-reported symptoms.

CHAPTER 5

Special Groups in the Police Service

There is some evidence to suggest that minorities working within organisations suffer adversely as a consequence of their minority status. In particular, sexual and racial discrimination and homophobic attitudes might be identified as presenting special problems for groups of individuals within working environments. This chapter looks at those features of the police working environment which might impact in a particular way on women, ethnic minorities and homosexual or lesbian officers and cause stress in such officers. The other significant minority group within the police service are the non-sworn or civilian personnel, and attention is also given to the special problems they may face.

Considerable research effort has been devoted to describing the police culture as a function of its domination by white males. Some detail is provided in the discussion given in Chapter 8. For present purposes, it is proposed to examine the relationship to stressor exposure and adverse reactions by virtue of membership of a minority group within this cultural milieu. There is, however, limited empirical investigation into these populations.

POLICEWOMEN

Research has indicated that policewomen are not only perceived differently by the public and male police officers but also themselves have different perspectives compared to policemen (Davis 1984; Jacobs 1987). Policewomen provide a particularly graphic example of the tensions presented by being a working woman. Two clashing images of the male and female domains are accentuated in an organisation such as the police force, dominated as it is by men and associated with danger and physicality. A woman in such an environment faces not only the occupational stresses of policing, but also the additional problems resulting from the organisation's treatment of her, as well as the behaviour and attitudes of her fellow officers. In order to describe and explain the sources of stress to which policewomen are exposed and the impact these may have, it is important to place their involvement within an historical and cultural context. Radford (1989) argues that the legacy of the history of policewomen's incorporation into the police service is vital when considering current attitudes and roles played by them today. The denial of policewomen's competence through their lack of physical strength and their limited access to specialisms and high rank contribute to a qualitatively different working environment for women officers. There is a growing body of research evidence from the United States (Martin 1979, 1980, 1989; Kroes 1982; Pogrebin 1986) and the United Kingdom (Bryant, Dunkerley and Kelland 1985; Jones 1986; Pope and Pope 1986; Brown and Campbell 1991a) which demonstrates that policewomen are not only excluded from the full range of police duties and deployments but also are subjected to sexual harassment. These factors obviously constitute significant and gender-specific sources of occupational stress. The outcomes for women officers have been claimed to be reduced job satisfaction, inhibition of their job motivation (Poole and Pogrebin 1988) and impediment of their promotion to higher rank (Halford 1987).

Despite facilitating legislation, both in America and in the United Kingdom, researchers have concluded that women officers are still disadvantaged by their gender and are not fully integrated into police forces (Jones 1986; Jacobs 1988; Martin 1989). The pressures associated with not being fully accepted and the experience of harassment or ostracism are significant sources of stress over and above those experienced by virtue of being a police officer.

Historical Context of Women Police Officers

Limitations on the range of functions women play in the police service are a reflection of attitudes towards women in general and specifically their role in law and order. A number of authors (Berg and Budnick 1986; Pogrebin 1986; Martin 1989) have documented that prior to 1972 in the United States, women police officers were originally used as matrons to deal with female offenders and then limited to clerical and juvenile division assignments. Despite the amendment to the Civil Rights Act guaranteeing women equality of opportunity in law enforcement careers, there is limited evidence of such equality in practice. Martin (1989) reported the results of a national questionnaire study of recruitment, selection and promotion policies for women officers in the United States. It was found that relative to their overall numbers, women officers were underrepresented in specialisms such as detective departments and did not have a proportional representation in higher ranks despite their growing presence in the service (about 10%). Pogrebin (1986) indicated that police departments are lagging behind both the requirements of legislation and the changing attitudes towards women at work generally, and more particularly public attitudes towards women in policing. So much so that in the absence of voluntary policies, the courts in the United States have required police departments to hire specific quotas of women officers in order to redress imbalances, and have also required them to promote women in proportion to their numbers in the department. Whilst Martin's (1989) review records some improvements, the conclusion of that review was that women were still not fully accepted or integrated within the United States police service.

The history of women's entry into the British police is marked by a gradual and reluctant extension of their role from strictly "female" duties to integration as police officers. Whilst the enabling legislation, the Sex Discrimination Act 1975, legally prescribes equal opportunities, as in the United States, the reality lags behind (Jones 1986). Bryant, Dunkerley and Kelland (1985) argued that women's role in the British police service was traditionally an extension of their maternal and caring roles: matron duties, searching and escorting female prisoners, working with children and juveniles. Their earliest role was to discourage "provocative loitering" near military centres during the 1914–18 war. Marwick (1977) explains this moral guardian role as deriving from the growth in social consciousness about prostitution and the demands of a licentious soldiery. Thus the British War Office gave permission for female police patrols.

After the First World War, this restricted role was extended to deal with women and children who were missing, ill, destitute or homeless and those living in immoral or unsavoury environments (Jones 1986). The Second World War heralded an expansion of duties to include driving and criminal investigation, but still within a separate "women's department" with its own rank structures, inspectorate and salary scales.

This partial role for women police remained the position in the United Kingdom until the Sex Discrimination Act of 1975. This Act states that it is unlawful for an employer to deny women access to opportunities for promotion or to other benefits or services or to subject them to any other type of detriment. Jones (1987a,b) has documented the considerable opposition, both from the British Police Federation and from the Association of Chief Police Officers, to the proposal that the police service should be included within the scope of the Sex Discrimination Act. The arguments forwarded for such opposition and resistance to the full integration of women officers have been:

(i)   the supposed physical and emotional inferiority of women;
(ii)   unsuitability of police work for women;
(iii)   lack of career mindedness amongst women;
(iv)   premature retirement of women through marriage or childbearing.

Porgrebin (1986) noted the same persistent perceptions amongst American policemen: ie that women lack physical strength and courage; that women are not dedicated careerists; and that their presence is prejudicial to discipline and cohesion within the service because of the potential of sexual and emotional entanglements. The origins of these perceptions lie in beliefs about women and their roles in society and the occupational self-image that men have about policing.

Empirical Evidence

There is a growing body of literature on the job motivations (Poole and Pogrebin 1988), leadership potential (Price 1974), and career progression of women officers (Martin 1989). However, there are relatively few well designed control studies of stress amongst female officers. The indications from available research suggest that female officers not only suffer stress from operational and organisational sources, but they are also exposed to gender-specific sources of stress. Kroes (1982) conducted clinical interviews with 34 American women officers whose average age was 34 years and average length of service 9 years. Their major sources of difficulty were associated with sexual harassment, ostracism and the grudging tolerance of fellow officers. Thereafter, sources of stress were similar to those of male officers, ie administrative policies and procedures, lack of support, line of duty crisis situations and emotional reactions to injury.

Wexler and Logan (1983) undertook an interview-based study with 25 of the 120 women officers in a California police department. Most officers mentioned organisational stressors, but the next most frequent stressors mentioned were those related to harassment in the form of questions about sexual orientation, or blatant anti-women comments.

The exposure of female officers to sexual harassment has been documented but less work is available that comments directly on the consequences. Gooch (1991) undertook a survey of 128 British police women from a single police force. Of these officers, 45% reported that they had been subjected to physical sexual harassment from male officers that caused them distress. Campbell and Brown (1992) explored the definitions of harassment given by policewomen themselves. The rates of experienced harassment and any adverse impact of harassment among a sample of women officers drawn from a British police force are given in Table 22.

Their research suggested that sexual harassment was a prevalent feature of policewomen's experience and that it had potentially adverse effects. Over 90% of women reported hearing comments about their own or other women's physical appearance and jokes about women, while 66% reported having been touched, pinched or groped and 6% said that they had been subject to a serious sexual assault. Women civilian support staff reported much lower

Table 22. Impact and frequency of sexual harassment by male police officers

	Policewomen		Traffic wardens		Civilian support staff	
	Frequency (%)	Impact (%)	Frequency (%)	Impact (%)	Frequency (%)	Impact (%)
Hearing jokes about women	95	32	84	25	88	42
Hearing comments about women's appearance	97	40	89	25	84	49
Hearing comments on own figure	92	80	72	46	54	66
Being touched, pinched, groped	66	87	28	60	43	84
Being seriously sexually assaulted	6	100	0	0	2	100

Source: Campbell and Brown (1992) .

rates of exposure to all the varieties of sexual harassment. The women who participated in this study indicated that, although their experiences had a negative impact on them, they would be unlikely to use formal grievance procedures to deal with their difficulties. It is striking that 11% of policewomen said that they had considered leaving the police service because of harassment. This compared with 9% of civilian support staff who had considered leaving for this reason.

Gutek and Morasch (1982) have suggested that "sex-role spillover" might account for the observed rates of sexual harassment in various occupational groups. They argue that when the sex ratio at work is skewed, there is a carry-over into the workplace of normative gender-based expectations for behaviours that are irrelevant or inappropriate to work settings. This is especially true if the numerically dominant gender also occupies the high status positions (Ott 1989). They suggested that gender identity becomes a more salient cognitive category than occupational aptitudes because:

(i)   gender identity is obvious and noticeable;
(ii)   men feel more comfortable in relating to women at work in the same manner that they relate to women as mothers or wives;
(iii)   women may feel more comfortable in conforming to male stereotypes of them; and
(iv)   the occupational demands of women are facilitated by the societal gender stereotype.

Stockdale (1991) has made a slightly different analysis of sexual harassment and relates it to the construction of personal identities as a product of social comparison processes. Where men define themselves to be different from and better than women, they denigrate women's skills and use sexual harassment as a mechanism both to support their prevailing view of incompetent women and to undermine women's confidence, thereby creating a self-fulfilling prophecy cycle. In other words, sexual harassment makes it difficult for women to achieve equal working relationships, which in turn adversely affects their performance and thus confirms men's view of women as incompetent.

Training has also been reported as a source of stress (Wexler and Logan 1983; Martin 1989). This was because male instructors were overtly hostile and the techniques chosen for physical restraint focused on those appropriate for upper body strength. These are inappropriate both for slighter men and for women officers. Wexler and Logan (1983) discussed the impact of slackening the emphasis on physical fitness during academy training for American women officers. Informal coddling of women, writes Martin (1989), negatively affects them, by permitting some to move to the next stage of recruit training without being fully prepared. This fosters an expectation that they can get along by being different. Such treatment, argues Martin, undermines the confidence of both male and female officers as well as creating unrealistic expectations amongst women officers themselves.

In a comparative study of distress among male and female officers in Montgomery County police, Pendergrass and Ostrove (1984) obtained self-reported symptoms from 352 male officers and 31 women. Two indices were constructed: a physiological index made up of items such as the occurrence of headaches, muscle tension, upset stomach; and a psychological index comprising measures of low self-esteem, isolation, cynicism. Overall, women officers reported higher rates of distress on both indices and also a higher rate of stress for police events than men. Overall, for any single item, the highest levels of distress for policemen were associated with fellow officers being killed in the line of duty and for women this was associated with killing someone in the line of duty.

These authors propose three alternative explanations for the reported differences: response bias, ie women may be more willing to reveal personal information; inhibition of women officers through organisational and cultural factors; and alleged deficiencies amongst women officers. Whilst empirical evidence is available from male police officers demonstrating their unfavourable attitudes towards women's competence (Vega and Silverman 1982; Balkin 1988), a number of studies evaluating policewomen's abilities to perform various patrol functions do not sustain their male colleagues' prejudices in practice (Block and Anderson 1974; Sherman 1975; Charles and Parsons 1978; Charles 1982).

The hypothesis concerning the greater likelihood of women admitting to personal difficulties is more difficult to disentangle. Few studies have attempted to differentiate sources and consequences of stress for men and women holding equivalent positions. Lowe and Northcott (1988) undertook a comparative investigation of 992 members of Canada's two main postal organisations. About half the sample were women. They used self-report measures of psychological and physiological symptoms associated with stress. They concluded that working conditions induced similar stress symptoms from both men and women, but that women reported higher levels. Predictors of distress were similar for both men and women—namely, ambiguous or conflicting demands on the job and the lack of variety or challenge of tasks at work. Significantly, the social role variable defined as the conflicts between the demands of home and work had almost no impact on distress experienced by either men or women workers. Amongst work-related stressors, the absence of friendly and helpful co-workers adversely affected women more than men.

Whilst this research does not specifically address the question of a response bias in women's symptom reporting rates compared to men, it does suggest that women respond to additional occupational stressors such as quality of interpersonal relations. The issue of a possible response bias remains ambiguous, but it does not negate the occurrence of organisational and cultural biases that militate against women in the police. Evidence from some British research supports this thesis.

Smith and Gray (1985) found evidence of sex discrimination and sexual harassment in the United Kingdom's Metropolitan police force. At the individual level, they found that female officers tended towards accommodating to the attitudes of their male colleagues and adjusted their career aspirations accordingly. Few women obtained entry to the Criminal Investigation Department and they were often denied access to specialisms such as the Dog Section, the Mounted Branch and Diplomatic Protection. Organisationally, the force was found to operate an unofficial policy to keep the proportion of women down to 10% on the grounds that women officers were unsuited to handle public order events or incidents where violence might be anticipated. It was noted that this was clearly contrary to the Sex Discrimination Act. These findings stimulated a joint study by the London Metropolitan Police Force and the Equal Opportunities Commission (Equal Opportunities Commission 1990). This study reviewed the criteria for entry into various policing specialisms and found that the Metropolitan Police were acting illegally by excluding women. Within the scope of their review, they carried out a small survey which found that women officers were more likely to work as custody or station officers or to work with women and young people.

The Equal Opportunities Commission funded additional research (Jones 1986) into the experiences of women officers. This study of 110 women and 244 men, in an average sized non-Metropolitan police force, concluded that informal practices did exclude women from a range of police duties. As a consequence, Jones concluded that women officers were limited in both the type and the amount of police experience to which they were exposed. This in turn affected their job satisfaction and inhibited their promotion prospects. Similarly Bryant, Dunkerley and Kelland (1985), in their survey of two British police forces, discovered an absence of women in Traffic Departments and CID and specialist units (eg Dog Handling and Scenes of Crime).

SENIOR WOMEN OFFICERS

Martin (1989) noted the absence of women from senior ranks in police departments in the United States. She reported statistics showing that women made up a smaller percentage of supervisors than the comparable figure for male officers; that the increase in the proportion of women in supervisory ranks between 1978 and 1986 was smaller than the overall increase in women's presence in policing; and that the higher the rank, the lower the proportion of females.

Adler (1990) found that between 1978 and 1986 the proportion of women sergeants in the United States increased from 1 to 3.7%, lieutenants increased from 0.7 to 2.5% and higher command ranks 0.5 to 1.4%. Adler suggests that promotional systems in the United States gave substantial weight to seniority which limited women's promotional chances, and supervisors' evaluations were found to discriminate against women.

The profile of women's rank distribution in the British police in 1990 was 4% of sergeants, 3% of inspectors, 3% of chief inspectors, 2% of superintendents and 2% of chief superintendents (Anderson, Brown and Campbell 1993). In 1993 there were only five women serving at the level of assistant chief constable. There are virtually no systematic studies of the stress experienced by senior women officers. Evidence has been culled from individual policewomen's experiences since, in the United Kingdom, there are so few occupying senior rank.

A recently retired woman commander from the London Metropolitan Police reflected thus on her promotion:

I think my sex was a handicap ... most officers having completed the [promotion] course rapidly get promoted to Commander or Assistant Chief Constable. It took me from 1979 to 1984 to get to the rank of Commander. If there's a gap in my progress, that would be it. (Henriques, 1988)

The same retired commander also commented, at an Equal Opportunities seminar held by the Police Federation of England and Wales, how different her experience had been on taking up a new post after retirement from the police. She described how her post-retirement experience contrasted with her experience in the police service. While in the police service, she felt that she had to re-establish her credentials each time she took up a new posting. In contrast, in the post taken up outside the police the starting assumption was that she had something of value to offer.

A more outspoken view of the difficulties for women in achieving high rank in the police was expressed by Halford (1987), who argued that senior women setting up initiatives find these projects handed to other (male) colleagues, that women are not represented at senior policy-making levels, and do not get short-listed for the very senior posts. Halford rhetorically asks: "Will the woman rock the boat, can she carry a shield, is it not 'odd'—in every sense of the word—that she wants to progress in her career?" Halford (1987) concludes: "Further advancement I suggest would need good luck, enormous resilience, great flexibility and superb coping strategy skills and being the solitary woman in a position of influence has its own very real disadvantages."

Joyce (1991) undertook an in-depth interview-based study of 6 male and 6 female British senior police officers. This study reported that the accounts of career progression given by senior policewomen are distinctive from those given by their male peers. One problem differentiating men's and women's career progress is the importance of operational experience for maintaining "credibility" for promotion. The particular difficulty for women officers is that often their career advancement is made via support roles or secondments to the Inspectorate or staff college. Joyce concludes:

whilst male and female officers alike may be subject to criticism, jokes and ridicule for non-operational status, women in particular may be subject to a harder task in maintaining operational credibility and avoiding the stigmatising effects of non-operational ghettoisation. Indeed, women may have to work hard at challenging attempts to ghettoise them and at maintaining operational credibility if they wish to achieve senior rank in operations, as opposed to support duties.

Kanter (1977) suggests that within organisations, men have more real power and greater opportunity for promotion. Blocked mobility, it is further suggested, leads to limited motivation, which in turn sets in motion a downward spiral of discouragement and potentially poor performances. Kanter (1977) also notes that numbers affect occupational behaviour, because minority representation takes on a token status. Token senior women face performance pressures due to their obvious visibility. They face isolation and can be forced into stereotypical roles because of the distortions of the dominant norms. Comments from one woman who achieved the most senior female rank in the British police illustrates some of these pressures: "I've learned to be more tactful and to keep my thoughts and aspirations under wraps" (Henriques 1988). Another senior woman writes: "the inability of some very senior men to cope with a woman of comparable rank is quite bewildering. There appears to be a strong but covert resentment or mistrust of the competence of a woman ... In some way the male seems threatened by the female ... and thus she is given little of the support, guidance or empathy which would be afforded a newly promoted male Assistant Chief Constable" (Halford 1987).

Comments from Joyce's (1991) in-depth study of senior women reiterate these themes. Here senior women officers discussed difficulties of managing their sexual identities and some of the problems related to the explicit and implicit assumptions about their sexuality. A male superintendent in Joyce's sample describes "blocking out", that is the lack of attention paid to women's views at meetings because they "don't really count", and makes the observation that it takes a very strong person to get through. Joyce also documents women's experiences of not revealing stress to male colleagues. One woman respondent explained: "they don't see my stress. I would rather die than let them see any sign of it because it would be trotted out from time to time ... [for men to] put the boot in." Support for senior women is much more likely to be found from lower ranked women officers, civilian employees or most often individuals outside the force. Joyce suggests that women may be reluctant to leave lower ranks because of this loss of solidarity since they are likely to suffer social isolation at higher levels in the organisation. There may also be a form of undermining carried out by women officers on their own sex. Malovich and Stake (1990) reported that women with high self-esteem were likely to respond to the problem of sexual harassment with surprise and indignation. Low-esteem women report fear and avoidance reactions. The high self-esteem women appeared to have little understanding of, or failed to give support to, women adversely affected by sexual harassment.

ETHNIC MINORITY OFFICERS

There is relatively little research available on the stress experienced by ethnic minority police officers, especially in the case of ethnic minority women. Sokoloff, Raffel-Price and Kuleshnyk (1992) noted that the experiences of the latter are typically subsumed under those of either women officers or ethnic minority officers in general. These researchers indicated that in the United States, ethnic minority women make up approximately 30% of all women officers whilst ethnic minority men comprise about 15% of all policemen. Martin (1989) suggests that the relatively large proportion of ethnic minority women officers in the United States is related to:

(i)   ethnic minority women viewing policing as an attractive occupational alternative, given limitations by racial discrimination and education to other job choices;

(ii)   ethnic minority women's history of occupational involvement with physical work and hence they may be less put off by this aspect of police work;

(iii)   recruitment policies being weighed such that employment of ethnic minority women fulfils both gender and racial quotas.

Ethnic minorities make up about 5% of the population in the UK (1981 Census). In the 42 forces in England and Wales (that is excluding the Metropolitan Police) the total number of police officers in 1990 was approximately 96 000, 11% of whom were women. Of the women officers just over 1% were from ethnic minorities. Ethnic minority men made up 0.1% of policemen (Anderson, Brown and Campbell 1993). The Metropolitan strength (1991 figures) was 28 440, of whom 2% were from the ethnic minorities. Ethnic minority women make up 3% of the comple- ment of female officers whilst ethnic minority men constitute 1.7% of the male officer complement.

Research conducted by the Policy Studies Institute (Smith 1983) included a questionnaire survey of Metropolitan Police officers. The respondent sample of 1770 included a subset of ethnic minor- ity officers. These ethnic officers, mostly Asian and Afro-Carib- bean, encountered particular difficulties because of racial preju- dice from members of the public and from their service colleagues. Just over half of the white officers (58%) thought relations between white and ethnic minority officers to be very good, whereas just over a third (37%) of ethnic minority officers reported this to be the case. Also 10% of the ethnic minority officers indicated their belief that promotion prospects were better for them than for white officers. This compared with 42% of white policemen thinking that promotion prospects were better for ethnic minority officers. A majority (68%) of those questioned in this survey thought that ethnic minority officers faced greater difficulties on the whole than their white colleagues. These difficulties were mostly thought to relate to dealing with ethnic groups in the community (51%), prejudice or racist remarks from the general public (17%), or non- acceptance by colleagues (5%). Research by Holdaway (Home Office 1990a) suggests that ethnic minority officers frequently hear comments on their ethnicity, face particular difficulties both from their colleagues and from the public and that these difficul- ties tended to be underestimated by senior officers.

Sokoloff, Raffel-Price and Kuleshnyk (1992) undertook an inter- view-based study of staff working in an American police acad- emy, 12 of whom were ethnic minority women, 7 white women, 3 Hispanic women and 3 white males. Results indicated that the question of discrimination was central to women officers' experi- ence in the police, in terms both of gender and of ethnicity. The ethnic minority women officers experienced a greater degree of

discrimination than other women, although this was not perceived to be any worse than in society at large. Rather, policing
was believed to provide alternatives not available elsewhere in an
environment where a narrow range of occupational options exist
for them. Of the little evidence available, women officers from
ethnic minorities suffer discrimination on two accounts by virtue
of their membership of two minority groupings.

A recent commentary by Neyroud (1992) suggested that for ethnic
minority women their experience of discrimination is more gen-
der- than racially based. Whilst there is no specific substantiating
evidence for the police service, it is the case that ethnic minority
women are least likely to achieve higher rank and are
overrepresented in general uniform patrol (Anderson, Brown and
Campbell 1993). The inference here is that rank and promotion are
two obvious ways of achieving rewards within the organisation
and they are least likely to be achieved by ethnic minority women.

In a small-scale survey (n = 67) of British ethnic minority school
children Doyle (1991) found that 45% thought they would make a
good police officer, and over half (52%) thought the police would
want them in the service. The most prevalent reason given for the
police not wanting them was racism. Unfortunately no comparison samples were used in this survey so it is difficult to establish
whether the ethnic minority children differed in their views from
non-minority children.

In a public attitude survey conducted on behalf of one British
police force, the Harris Research Centre (1992) reported that of the
102 ethnic minority general public sample, over three-quarters
indicated they would approve if a family member joined the
police—the same proportion as in the main sample of 956 general
public respondents. Ethnic minority respondents were much
more likely to say that ethnic minority recruitment could help to
improve relations between the police and public than the main
sample (16% compared to 1%). Almost all of the ethnic minority
respondents (91%) thought it important for this police force to
recruit ethnic minorities compared with 71% from the main sample.
Just over half the ethnic minority respondents (51%) thought racist
attitudes were a very or quite serious problem compared with 22%
of the main sample.

Cashmore (1991) has described the experiences over time of some black officers as their numbers have increased in American police departments. Officers engaged in community policing of ethnic minority ghetto areas and those officers who achieved senior ranks were noted to have suffered adversely from negative attitudes and prejudice.

CIVILIAN PERSONNEL

In England and Wales, 193 000 personnel were employed within the police service in 1990. Of these, 65.3% were police officers, 24.2% civilians, and 8% special constables (ie voluntary part-time police officers) and 2.5% were traffic wardens (Audit Commission 1992). A study by the British Association of Chief Police Officers noted that numbers of civilian personnel in the police force have progressively increased since the 1940s (Association of Chief Police Officers 1980). Their report documents that during the Second World War, civilian personnel were recruited into the police thus establishing the principle of civilianising certain police functions. After the war, the practice continued. In 1949 the Oaksey Committee established the rationale for civilianisation in support functions to release police officers for operational duties. The employment of civilian staff has grown numerically since that time and expanded into an increasing range of police functions. The Home Office Circular 114/1983 on "Manpower effectiveness and efficiency in the police service" states that the Home Secretary will not normally approve increases in establishment if police officers are occupying posts which could properly and more economically be filled by civilians.

The ACPO report referred to above concluded that little attempt had been made to give civilians a proper sense of status or a career structure and that their special functions and the demands made on them go unrecognised.

The types of work undertaken by civilian staff, in addition to clerical and administrative work, include scenes of crime work, finger printing, photography, scientific examination of road accidents, control room operation, training, computing and other technical support. A review of forces conducted by the ACPO working group indicated that the majority of civilians are employed by the respective Police Authority and most adopted the County Council's personnel practices and discipline procedures in managing civilian staff.

The gender breakdown revealed in a detailed examination of the civilian complement of one force (Highmore 1991) showed not only that 65% of civilian staff are women, but that the majority are represented at the lower ends of the pay scales.

There have been indications of problems with the management of civilian staff. Mason (1988) reported an estimated civilian staff turnover of between 25 and 30% in the South East of England. This high level of wastage was attributed in part to the lack of defined career structures and variations in gradings between forces. Pay differentials for the same posts in different forces are said to contribute to low morale. Also civilians working alongside and performing the same duties as police officers may resent the pay differential between them and police officers. Another factor cited by Mason (1988) was the attitudes of police officers towards civilians, which can be condescending or undermining. Whilst not engaged in a front line policing role, civilians are increasingly being deployed in operational capacities. One such is that of control room operator or dispatcher. These staff are deployed to receive the incoming radio and telephone messages and to dispatch and support police personnel to deal with the arising situations. Sewell and Crew (1984) note that little attention has been given to the experience of stress by non-sworn police personnel. They note, in the American context, a number of potential sources of stress for civilian dispatchers: their perception of second class citizen status; inadequate training which tends to be on the job rather than formal training programmes; the volume of radio traffic; pressures associated with rapid decision-making; equipment problems and breakdowns; confined working environments; and dealing with stressed citizens.

In a study of the stress experienced by police and civilian dispatchers working in two English forces, one metropolitan and one provincial, Funnelle, Brown and Woolfenden (1991) found relatively few differences in the rate of exposure to stressors or

experience of distress between police and civilian staff (Table 23).
The most likely sources of stress were equipment failure or breakdown, having to deal with a call in which an officer required
assistance, and handling calls dealing with sexual offences. In
common with operational officers, communications staff also
reported that staff shortages, lack of resources, work overload,
lack of consultation or communication were potential sources of
stress.

Table 23. Control room civilian personnel's versus police officers' average stressor exposure and felt stress scores

Police force one	Civilians	Police
Exposure to police operational stressors	4.6	5.9
Felt stress from police operational stressors	9.7	12.0
Exposure to organisational stressors	12.8	17.3
Felt stress from organisational stressors	30.9	38.1
Police force two	Civilians	Police
Exposure to police operational stressors	3.1	2.7
Felt stress from police operational stressors	5.1	4.9
Exposure to organisational stressors	7.6	9.0
Felt stress from organisational stressors	14.5	19.2

Source: Funnelle, Brown and Wolfenden (1991).

The other significant area in which civilian personnel are deployed is in traffic warden duties. Richman (1983), in an ethnographic study of British traffic wardens, documented their introduction and incorporation within the police force. Their role is to assist in the regulation of car parking and movement of traffic. Richman posits that no similar group has attracted comparable opprobrium, ridicule or sustained insults. From the fieldwork of his study, he documents the hostility and aggression wardens can face when dealing with the public. Threats and abuse were regular features of their daily encounters. Women wardens were told that they would be better employed looking after their children or told derisively to go back to their council houses. He found that men were not subjected to these specific insults. Richman suggested that for car drivers, especially men, it was felt to be inappropriate for women wardens to exert punitive power over them. This feeling was exacerbated if the incident happened in front of other people. Interestingly, female traffic wardens were more likely to report that women, or younger motorists, exhibited aggression towards them whereas male traffic wardens indicated that men or middle-aged motorists were the more aggressive.

From a small-scale survey of sexual harassment conducted amongst traffic wardens in one British police force, Funnelle (1992) discovered that the most likely perpetrators of such harassment were members of the public. One in three traffic wardens agreed this was the case. Women wardens reported that their most common experiences of harassment were hearing comments about women in general or about their own appearance (see Table 22). Most dealt with these by trying to ignore the comments although a proportion reported the experiences as having an adverse impact on them.

An increasing number of police forces in the UK are using civilian members of staff to work as station duty officers dealing with the public's enquiries made to the police station. One metropolitan force undertook a small-scale study of 24 civilian staff and 42 police officers working on these duties (Mitchell 1991). Over 70% of all staff indicated that work overload, staffing levels, staffing shortages and inability to take a meal break were amongst the most frequently occurring stressors. Working in isolation was reported three times as often by civilian staff compared with police officers and was the only stressor which occurred at a significantly greater rate in the civilian group.

Lack of support, boredom at work, lack of consultation or communication, criticism by the public, lack of training, conflicts between home and work, criticism by the media, problems of staffing levels, demands of work impinging on the home, were all reported as having an adverse impact if experienced by front office staff, both police officers and civilians. When comparing stressors experienced by operational police officers with those experienced by the front office staff, the latter reported a lower rate of exposure and less adverse reactions (Mitchell 1991).

HOMOSEXUAL AND LESBIAN OFFICERS

There is a dearth of research on the stress associated with being a homosexual police officer. The problems experienced by these officers have been highlighted in Britain through the formation of the Lesbian and Gay Police Association (LAGPA). A major objective of this Association is to have sexual orientation included in police forces' equal opportunities policy statements. This would then enable officers to have access to grievance procedures should they feel they have been subject to discriminatory treatment. Research examining such treatment tends to be sparse and therefore reliance has to be placed on personal accounts. One such account (Hunt 1991) described the immense emotional trauma experienced as a consequence of a homosexual relationship becoming public knowledge. The officer described how the response of the organisation was to transfer the two officers concerned to vice squad attachments, and to require them to have medical examinations. Another personal account (O'Neill 1990) describes the harassment experienced by an officer whose colleagues thought he was homosexual, resulting in the officer resigning from the force.

Burke (1992) discusses the conventional and parochial morality of officers within the British police and argues that this stands at the opposite end of a political and social attitude spectrum from the stance espoused by the homosexual community. Given the observations of a number of commentators on the machismo of the police canteen culture, then homosexuality, argues Burke, not only threatens the masculinity of police officers but also threatens their sense of mission. This mission is seen as being the guardians of public morality: homosexuals are seen as threats to the existing social order. Burke further suggests that to understand homosexuality is intellectually demanding and requires more time and effort than most police officers are prepared to find. This predisposes officers to operate on the basis of stereotypes which in the case of the police is compounded because they tend to be involved in criminal aspects of homosexuality (O'Neill 1990). According to Burke (1992) this has the important effect of not challenging the stereotypes of the effeminate or butch homosexual and the aggressive dungareed woman or grim grey spinster. The result is to preserve an intolerance of those with homosexual orientations because the acceptance or condoning of homosexuality would represent a threat to the integrity of the service.

The notion of contagion or contamination is prevalent amongst anti-homosexual attitudes. Thus an editorial in *Police Review* (18 January 1991) stated: "homosexuality particularly in men still offends a great many people who view it as immoral, unnatural or irreligious. And there will be a certain amount of unease. 'If I show sympathy for the problems faced by gays, will I myself be branded homosexual.'" The *Police Journal* prefaced Burke's (1992) article on homosexuality with a commentary that included the following: "most police officers, as with heterosexual members of society generally, have no sympathy with those who engage in homosexual conduct, indeed some find it distasteful in the extreme, but this should not be allowed to affect in any way the manner in which they carry out their duties". The homosexual officer, male or female, unlike an ethnic minority member is not necessarily "visible" to his or her colleagues. Coping covertly in an environment in which there is a fallacious and inaccurate stereotypic conception of homosexuality is likely to be problematic and difficult.

Henderson (1981), commenting on the attitudes of American police officers towards homosexuals, writes: "homosexuality is both repulsive and threatening to male police who have been taught to value their masculinity and heterosexuality above most other traits. It is repulsive because it clearly violates the majority norms, and it is threatening because an individual may have latent homosexual tendencies." O'Leary (1981), in a report which was presented to the US Commission on Civil Rights hearing concerning police practices and preservation of Civil Rights, suggested that police officers not only ignored assaults on, and harassment of, homosexual citizens but also subjected suspects to abuse, extortion or entrapment. O'Leary argues that one way such attitudes and practices against other minorities have been lessened is by ensuring that members of these minorities are well represented in police forces. However, because of the problems faced by homosexual officers, both male and female, in "coming out" publicly, then this minority remains invisible.

The situation in the United Kingdom is not entirely different. Gash (1992), a member of the Police Federation of England and Wales, writes: "Like many police officers, I came from a background where homosexuality has always been abhorred, and as far as I was concerned, homosexuals were people who practised unnatural sex and interfered with small children. The males were pansies and the women sexual misfits. My police experience helped to reinforce these attitudes, because the only time we were in contact with gays was to prosecute them for various offences." However, having attended a workshop organised by LAGPA, Gash comments on the courage of officers who publicly profess their sexuality and concludes: "all my discussions with LAGPA members convince me that they will do more to change the hostile attitudes of their colleagues, and get rid of the myths and stereotyping, by being open than we can achieve simply by stating our belief in equality". However, coming out presents many conflicts and anxieties for the homosexual officer.

In one of the very few studies of homosexuality in the police Antony (1991) discusses coming out at some length. Antony undertook in-depth interviews with 15 homosexual police officers. None were explicit about their sexual orientation when joining the police, some had not identified or accepted their homosexuality. Several of Antony's respondents described the stress associated with coming to terms with their sexual orientation. Fear of discovery acted as a significant blight on the lives of most respondents, who talked of being petrified or frightened. The stress involved in deciding to come out at work is also a considerable burden. Those that had often did so by force of circumstances. One officer had to supply an alibi that compromised his personal life, in order to refute an unrelated allegation. Another was unable to cope at work because he had broken up with his partner and decided to account for his poor work performance by telling the truth about his situation.

Telling friends and colleagues, even if they had not already guessed, is reported as extremely stressful. There is much concern expressed for officers who chose not to come out. Antony comments: "sometimes, those who are not out are more badly affected by a homophobic culture than those who are out. Those affected worst are those who are actively working to disguise their homosexuality." Officers may have to repeat the coming out process because of career moves. Whilst the level of homophobia at work locations is not uniform, officers describe the uncertainty that is felt on arrival at a new location. After asking if they had experienced discrimination or harassment, Antony reports a general absence of individual or institutionalised discrimination. Whilst officers gave examples of unpleasant graffiti and cruel jokes, the respondents felt much was due to ignorance and was often inadvertent. This response is strikingly similar to reactions to racist jokes by ethnic minority officers or sexual harassment by women officers.

Promotion or applications for specialist appointments may be compromised if officers believe their sexual orientation will be discovered through vetting procedures, and a posting such as youth work might attract public opprobrium if the sexual orientation of the officer were known. Antony's respondents mentioned some specific objections that police officers express with reference to homosexual colleagues. These include concerns over prisoner handling. This issue was met with some outrage by the respondents who were offended by the insinuation that they would be sexually aroused or responsive in such situations. Antony notes: "there is also consternation at the homophobic stereotype of a gay person as being a totally sexual being. Some of the people I interviewed told me that they are not especially sexually active, and they resent the inference that the physical expression of their sexual orientation would ever become evident in the ordinary course of non-sexual events."

A point made by many of the officers in Antony's sample was that if the person passes "the good copper" test he or she may be allowed to have a deviant characteristic such as being homosexual. Thus so long as officers are perceived to be effective police officers, and this applies to any individual who appears to be different, then they may be accepted within the organisation. However, Antony's respondents imply that only one area of difference tends to be tolerated, so officers are pressured to conform to other demands of the culture.

SUMMARY

Given the dominance of white males among serving police officers, members of minority groups might expect to experience additional stressors over and above those experienced by the majority group. It is clear that women, ethnic minority and homosexual officers may face a good deal of harassment and discrimination from within the organisation.

Several authors have drawn attention to the coping strategies used by minorities, whether defined by gender, race or sexual orientation. Many try to ignore the comments or behaviour of their fellow officers; some regard the comments as due to ignorance or thoughtlessness and try to minimise the impacts. There is growing evidence that harassment can lead to victims suffering stress symptoms. Indeed Mezey and Rubenstein (1992) have documented cases of Post Traumatic Stress Disorder (PTSD) in three victims of sexual harassment. Clinical evidence was presented at subsequently successful Industrial Tribunals where claimants were awarded damages for their suffering. A number of claims by police officers suffering racial discrimination have also attracted significant financial settlement.

The police occupational culture has been envisaged as having a number of undesirable characteristics. Awareness of these characteristics is important in order to mitigate the stressors that may impinge on members of minority groups within the police service. Senior women and officers from ethnic minorities in particular suffer from their progressively fewer numbers in the higher echelons of the organisation.

Much of the available evidence on stressor exposure from minority groups is based on personal accounts or anecdotal sources. This nevertheless does indicate that stressors impinging on women supervisors and ethnic minority officers are, in some respects, qualitatively different from those affecting more junior women or white counterparts.

There is also little formal evidence of the distress experienced by gay police officers. Many of the available findings are reliant on personal testimonies. These suggest that gay officers are subjected to harassment and that making their sexual orientation public can be particularly distressing for such officers.

Civilian staff are becoming an increasingly important element of police personnel. Those functioning in substitute operational roles such as dispatcher suffer equally as much from stressors as do their police counterparts.

CHAPTER 6

Strategies for Change:
The Individual

STRATEGIES

There are three principal strategies that police forces can adopt for dealing with the problem of the overstressed member of staff:

- *Primary prevention*. The two main approaches here are (a) to attempt to eliminate or reduce the sources of stress or (b) to select recruits who will be relatively immune to any adverse effects of stress because of personal or other factors.
- *Secondary intervention*. This might include debriefings following exposure to traumatic events and access to advice or help before any psychological problems have a chance to develop.
- *Tertiary intervention*. This would encompass all those arrangements designed to support or aid officers who are suffering from psychological problems. Such efforts would include the provision of counselling services, access to convalescent homes, medical discharges from the service.

Firth and Shapiro (1986) advance the argument that working with individuals suffering from acknowledged distress is a more effective way of approaching stress management than preventive work among non-stressed members of the workforce. They acknowledge the gains of preventive work but suggest that these are actually quite small, as revealed by properly controlled evaluative studies. In their own study of 40 managerial/professional workers seeking help for clinically severe job-related distress, most clients achieved positive outcomes as a consequence of therapy and returned to their previous levels of job performance. The problems involved centred on relationship difficulties and low self-esteem, both of which are largely interpersonal concepts and less amenable to organisational structural intervention.

Cox, Boot and Cox (1988) on the other hand propose a problem-solving approach set within the context of general systems theory. This posits that organisational structures and processes must not only be taken into account when viewing individuals' capacities but also in themselves may generate stress. Job-related distress in their study of teachers was found to be associated with lack of training and career development, physical working environment, size of school and length of line management. They argue that it is cost-effective to prevent the occurrence of stressful situations at work or at least to reduce the frequency with which they occur.

Brown and Campbell (1991b) discuss these issues in relation to the needs of the police and other emergency services. They conclude that these two approaches are not mutually exclusive and that individual curative therapy is both desirable and necessary. Alkus and Padesky (1981) conclude that whilst intervention models are popular, they tend to help only those officers who develop serious stress-related problems. They suggest that prevention models are preferable because they are cost-effective in that they do not require officers to admit they are in difficulty, and also may have knock-on effects in the area of interpersonal skill development. However, Alkus and Padesky (1981) point out that it may be organisationally convenient to focus on the failure of individuals when it is in fact structural features that actually caused, or contributed to, some operational error or management misjudgement.

There are numerous ways in which mismanagement of the stressed officer can occur. The most obvious of these is that no one, including perhaps even the officer in question, notices when an individual is distressed. This is perhaps most common if there has been an insidious and slow onset of the problem over a number of months or years. The second most common mistake is then that of conceptualising the individual officer's problem as one of discipline or "laziness". This might obviously result in an officer being subjected to disciplinary procedures rather than being offered psychological help.

There are financial implications of both the management and the mismanagement of the stressed officer. The costs of mismanagement will include:

(i)   absenteeism;
(ii)   lack of efficiency at work;
(iii)   "mistakes" or errors of judgement;
(iv)   inappropriate premature retirement or discharge;
(v)   poor morale;
(vi)   decreasing attractiveness of the job to possible recruits.

The benefits of managing the problem of stress effectively would potentially include improved morale and retention rates and reduced sickness absence. Some of the varieties of interventions that are available to police forces are detailed in the rest of this chapter.

SELF-HELP

There is a great variety of material available for individuals to use in the self-management of stress and distress. This ranges from manuals and books to audiotapes and videotapes. The self-help books generally invite the reader to take stock in various ways by completing "stress checklists" or prioritising values/objectives and such like. They then offer a variety of methods for achieving a reduction in experienced stress. These generally include elements such as reappraisal of belief systems, identifying sources of stress, increasing personal resources and supports, symptom-reduction techniques and physical care. The popularity of the self-help approach is demonstrated by the sales figures for books about self-control of stress. Anecdotally, individuals often report that they have achieved considerable insight or guidance from such texts. However, there is no simple way of assessing the overall usefulness of a self-help approach compared to other approaches and such a comparison would not, anyway, be particularly helpful.

INFORMAL SUPPORT NETWORKS, PEER SUPPORT AND PEER COUNSELLING

The police organisation can also facilitate the use of informal support sources such as spouses or colleagues. This can be done either explicitly, by setting up self-help groups, or implicitly, by fostering a particular ethos within the organisation.

Some authors who have written about the role of spouses as support have tended to assume that this can almost be taken for granted as being an integral part of the "job description" of a police officer's spouse (cf Young 1984). In most instances it is also assumed that the police officer is male and that the spouse is therefore a woman with available time and energy for mopping up any emotional overspill from her husband's job. No mention is made of policewomen's spouses and whether they too would be expected to perform such a role. In the United Kingdom at least two police forces are known to be encouraging spouse counselling as a resource.

Neidig, Russell and Seng (1992) note the recommendations made to a congressional hearing on the stress experienced by police officers and their families. It was proposed that police departments should provide education and family support services. The family support and family advocacy services mandated by the US Department of Defense were felt to offer appropriate models for the police service. In an empirical investigation, Neidig, Russell and Seng (1992) discovered that there were higher rates of violence inflicted by police officers on their partners, if the officers worked midnight rather than day shifts or were working on narcotics units rather than other assignments. These authors were unable to unravel specific causal links from their results, but nevertheless concluded that the rate of domestic violence amongst police families was sufficiently worrying as to demand some commitment to a treatment and prevention programme.

Other informal, or semi-informal, networks of support may be provided by force chaplains, Police Federation representatives or supervisory officers. One of the main disadvantages of using informal networks or peer support as a tool for the management of stress-related conditions is that such arrangements tend to be ad hoc, patchy and inconsistent.

Peer counselling refers to the use of police officers themselves as the counsellors for their colleagues. Officers are usually volunteers or those occupying specific counselling-related jobs such as Union representatives or welfare/personnel officers. These officers are given some kind of brief training in the fundamental elements of counselling and counselling skills. This normally includes: (i) how to form the right kind of trusting relationship; (ii) active listening skills to facilitate the exploration of the problem by the troubled officer; and (iii) helping the officer to examine the options for dealing with the problem and choosing between them. Peer counselling systems may be informal or formal in their organisation. They usually have relatively modest objectives of containment and support.

One of the advantages of a peer counselling system is claimed to be the degree of understanding and fellow feeling that another officer can have because of belonging to the same organisation and having been exposed to similar experiences. A further advantage reported for peer counselling is the ease of consultation and the lack of perceived stigma that might be attached to consultation with a professional helper. It might be the case that police officers would more readily make use of a peer counselling system than a professional counselling service because of these considerations. It has also been suggested that peer counselling should be supported on grounds of utility and economy since full-time professional counsellors are a relatively scarce and expensive resource (McDonald 1989).

However, the difficulties associated with a peer counselling scheme may be thought to outweigh the possible advantages (Brown and Campbell 1991b). Because of the hierarchical nature of police forces, it is difficult for a truly "peer" system to work. It is most unlikely that senior officers would consult junior officers and vice versa. It is therefore debatable whether a "peer" system is possible in a hierarchical and disciplined institution. Confidentiality can also be a problem. If officers are consulting their peers as counsellors within police premises then it might be difficult to preserve confidentiality about who is using the service. Officers may also be reluctant to be entirely open with their peers, either because of any disciplinary implications of admissions about their behaviour or because they might find themselves directly supervising or being supervised by that same person later in their career. The use of peer counsellors is not feasible for officers who have been suspended from duty and are facing disciplinary hearings. Such officers, in the United Kingdom, are prohibited from contact with fellow officers and from entering police premises. There is therefore the problem of a possible conflict of interests and loyalties with resultant difficulties about role boundaries that will potentially bedevil a peer counselling system. A peer counselling system would also require some mechanism for monitoring, supervision, and on-going training. The recommendation from the Joint Working Party on Organisational Health and Welfare report (1987) on counselling for police officers in the United Kingdom was that peer counselling was not appropriate at present and that professional counselling schemes should be set up before any peer counselling schemes are considered. Hillas and Cox (1986) stated a similar view rather forcefully in their report on PTSD when discussing the psychological support that could be offered to officers: "There is no room for the enthusiastic and well meaning amateur within the Police Force."

The informal support and counselling provided by force chaplains and others has sometimes been formalised into a structured "in-house" counselling provision. Police forces which have adopted this strategy usually ask for volunteers or recommended individuals. They therefore have a combined system of some peer counsellors and some designated counsellors such as force chaplains, welfare officers, Federation representatives and staff from the Personnel Office.

The majority of British police forces have some full-time welfare officer, although the role of welfare officer is often not very clearly defined (National Welfare Officers' Conference 1987). The Joint Working Party on Organisational Health and Welfare (1987) suggested that the role of the welfare officer should be: (i) to provide information and advice to management and the workforce on all aspects of any counselling scheme; (ii) to act as a sorting office to direct those with problems to the most appropriate source of assistance; and (iii) to provide practical advice and first line counselling to officers seeking help. One difficulty with the concept of a welfare officer is that there are associated paternalistic notions, of being almost a "charity" case. Also because the welfare officer is seen as an integral part of the managerial system (and in many instances is an ex-police officer) there can be a reluctance on the part of the individual officer to approach the welfare officer with the admission of being in difficulty.

The role of the force medical officer varies between forces with respect to responsibility for an involvement with counselling provision. Most usually the duties of the force medical officer involve routine medical checks and medical assessments in cases of early retirement on health grounds.

CAREER COUNSELLING

Officers who perceive their work as boring or meaningless, who are overworked or underworked, or who feel that their skills are not being adequately utilised are likely to experience stress as a result. Career counselling can facilitate the appropriate placement of officers so that there is some chance of meshing the needs of the organisation with the skills and interests of the individuals employed in it. This topic will be further examined in Chapter 7. Retirement counselling or pre-retirement preparation courses are also provided by some police forces.

PHYSICAL FITNESS PROGRAMMES

Most stress management programmes include educational elements which help officers to identify stress both in themselves and in those they are supervising. In a small-scale evaluation of a course in relaxation training for sergeants and field commanders in one British police force, Brown (1989) found that 80% of those participating reported it to be useful both in managing their own stress levels and in their managerial role.

General health and fitness initiatives have been undertaken by a number of forces. For example, one British police force has been testing officers by using a computerised fitness testing system, by introducing healthy menus in the canteens and by providing health education lectures. Other forces have used mobile exhibitions with information provided on diet, exercise, smoking and fitness.

However, it has been difficult to find conclusive evidence for the positive impact of physical fitness training on police performance. Hardy, Parfitt and Baker (1989) examined the relationships between physical fitness, psychological coping and stress in a sample of British police officers. They undertook a detailed examination of the impact of physical fitness and psychological coping by police officers engaged in operating a computer-based command and control system. Three measures of physical fitness were selected and one measure of psychological well-being. Their data indicated rather poorer mental health amongst their police sample than samples from other occupational groups. Job satisfaction was the strongest predictor of mental health for both policemen and policewomen; this was a better predictor than the physical fitness variables. They concluded that a supportive supervisory environment was probably rather more likely to enhance well-being than was a physical fitness regime per se. In a small experimental study, Norris, Carroll and Cochrane (1990) looked at the effect of different physical fitness regimes on psychological well-being. Volunteers joined either a regular running or a weightlifting programme. Although preliminary results appeared to show some association between improved physical fitness, psychological well-being and work performance, the authors concluded that the nature of this association was still unclear. They suggested that "no one simple factor is at work ... benefits accruing from fitness programmes come from a variety of sources".

PROFESSIONAL COUNSELLING SERVICES

A number of police forces have now instituted some kind of professional counselling service which is available to police officers, and sometimes also to civilian staff (Stratton 1980; Reese and Goldstein 1986). Sewell (1986) estimated that 20–25% of law enforcement agencies in the United States had some kind of stress management programmes available to their workforce. In Delprino and Bahn's (1988) study of the extent and nature of psychological services in United States police departments, more than half of all the departments contacted were using some kind of psychological services. Officer counselling was a common feature of such services.

The rationale for having a professional counselling service rather than an in-house or peer counselling system is convincing. One of the main strengths of a professional service is its ability to ensure confidentiality for the users of the service. In addition, the use of professional psychologists or counsellors means that a better service can be provided with the potential for more effective interventions, knowledge of other agencies and services, and the possibility of referral to other agencies when that is deemed to be appropriate.

More than half of British police forces have had some kind of independent professional counselling service available for their workforce since the late 1980s. Some of these forces have combined this with an in-house peer counselling scheme which is either an alternative to the professional counselling or the first port of call with referral on to the professional counsellor in those cases judged to be beyond the competence of the in-house service.

Some police forces have attempted to specify under what conditions an employee might use the professional service. For example, at least one British police force retained a professional counsellor for those officers who experienced distress as a direct result of experiences connected with their police duties. Problems of a more "personal" nature such as marital difficulties or alcohol misuse problems unrelated to work were expected to be referred to the local existing agencies. However, in this particular force, these criteria were found to be too strict and were then modified so that any officer whose functioning at work was seriously impaired, for whatever reason, was able to be referred to the professional counsellor.

In British police forces, the Home Office guidelines on police counselling services suggest that the force medical officer should be the channel through which all referrals to the professional counselling service are made. Some police forces have set up the force welfare officer as such a channel. In most instances there are also provisions made for self-referral or referral via supervisory officers. The most usual reason for having some kind of official channel is for monitoring and auditing purposes.

While attendance at any professional counselling service is usually on a voluntary basis, there are some occasions when police staff may be directed to attend by either the force medical officer or a supervisory officer. Because of the disciplined nature of the police service, this is often perceived by the individual officer to be compulsory attendance. There are times when it may be that officers would benefit from mandatory counselling or at least mandatory psychological screening or debriefing. For example, any officer involved in a serious traumatic event might routinely have a debriefing session or be assessed by a professional psychologist. The argument for such mandatory attendance is twofold. First, no stigma is attached to attendance, and second the potential experience of psychological distress is normalised and seen to be accepted by the institution. Other occasions when mandatory counselling might be appropriate are when officers are perceived to be a danger either to themselves or to others or when officers are facing serious disciplinary charges.

It has been assumed that the financial costs of providing a professional counselling service can be offset against the savings made in a number of areas. It is suggested that counselling will reduce absenteeism, improve effectiveness, improve retention of staff, improve morale and prevent future psychological problems by providing education in stress identification and reduction. However, assessing any preventive effects of counselling is a very difficult evaluation task.

The UK Home Office Science and Technology Group (1989), via the Police Requirements Support Unit, has surveyed the availability of organisational health and welfare facilities within the individual police forces of England and Wales and the Royal Ulster Constabulary. Only two forces did not have any counselling facilities. Of the 44 forces, 27 provided the services of a professional counsellor both for general counselling and for traumatic incident counselling. A further 7 used a professional counsellor for traumatic incidents but no other purpose. The welfare officer acted as a counsellor in 33 of the forces.

Estimates of how many officers used these facilities varied widely with some forces reporting that as few as two officers used them whereas the Royal Ulster Constabulary estimated that several hundred officers were involved. In the London Metropolitan Police the figure given was 1800. The majority of forces stated that their officers were trained in stress identification and that they had a force working party on organisational health.

Martin (1990) carried out a survey to identify what British and Dutch officers respectively saw as stressful incidents and to look at what effects they reported such incidents had upon them. Eleven British police forces yielded a total of 206 replies and 34 Dutch police officers responded. The various types of incidents that officers were exposed to were recorded and could be grouped into:

(i)   Violent death experiences/murder.
(ii)   Serious grievous bodily harm.
(iii) Direct assault on themselves.
(iv)   Multi-fatal and fatal accidents.
(v)   Public order experiences.
(vi)   Arrest involving actual bodily harm or assault.

Officers were also asked if they would consider using a Force Counselling Scheme if they had been distressed by a critical or traumatic incident. In reply 53% said that they would consider using such a service. Among those who said that they would not use such a service, the main reasons cited were that they thought that they would be able to handle it alone, or that they would lack confidence in the system, or they would prefer to use their own support networks. Other reasons given included a lack of trust in the confidentiality of the system, a belief that using such a service would be detrimental to their career and that it would be unacceptable to the police service culture. The majority of Martin's respondents (85%) were sceptical about the possibility of keeping anything confidential in the police service.

Martin also posed the question of whether officers thought that it would be in their own best interests to have a mandatory system of referral to independent counsellors after involvement in a traumatic or critical incident. The response showed that 61% thought that it would be for the best if there were such a mandatory scheme, with only 31% disagreeing. However, feelings about mandatory schemes were complex, with officers perceiving that there would be both advantages and disadvantages in such a set up. Interestingly nearly 75% of officers thought that a mandatory counselling scheme for traumatic incidents would overcome some of the resistance that police officers report to seeking professional help. Officers were more likely to say that they would elect to use a counselling scheme following a major disaster and least likely to do so after a public order event. Two-thirds said that they might use such a scheme following an arrest which involved actual bodily harm.

Anderson and Bauer (1987), in discussing from a North American perspective how shooting incidents should be dealt with, suggest that mandatory counselling serves two purposes: (i) it establishes that managers see the need for help as "normal" and not as a sign of weakness, and (ii) it overcomes the problem that if officers are questioned about post-shooting counselling in court later that it cannot be seen as indicative of any personal instability but as routine departmental policy. Anderson and Bauer (1987) have suggested that in order for professional counsellors to have credibility with officers it may be necessary for them to be exposed to routine police work. They also assert, although without providing any evidence, that achieving credibility might be more difficult for female than for male counsellors. However, this assumption seems predicated on the notion of a normative male officer.

Counsellors are in a unique position of being the recipients of information about all the different parts of an organisation (Megranahan 1989). They are thus able to provide feedback to managers about possible areas of conflict or concern and to make constructive suggestions for change. Megranahan (1989) suggests a number of general principles which should underpin a workplace counselling system. These are listed in Table 24.

Research has been reported on an in-house counselling service offered by the British postal service to their employees. Psychological problems had become the second most common reason in this organisation for medical retirement (Allison, Cooper and

Table 24. Principles which should underpin a workplace counselling scheme

---

1.   Any counselling service needs to have the support of top management in order to be accepted and survive

2.   A written policy statement of overall philosophy concerning the health and well-being of employees ... should be available. This creates a positive climate in which employees can seek help

3.   Managers and supervisors should be trained to identify employees with problems at an early stage and know how to confront them and make referral to the counsellor

4.   Access to the counselling service should be available to all staff at all locations

5.   The service should be credible in the eyes of the employers, managers, trade unions, and employees

6.   Confidentiality should be explicitly stated, accepted, and understood by everyone

7.   A continuation of care should be available, which includes referral and follow-up

8.   The emphasis should be on self-referral

9.   The counselling service should be independent of any specific or single treatment centre

10. A system should exist for evaluating the counselling service

---

Source: reproduced by permission from M. Megranahan (1989). Counselling in the workplace. In W. Dryden, D. Charles-Edwards and R. Woolfe (Eds), *Handbook of Counselling in Britain*. London: Tavistock/Routledge.

Reynolds 1989). Specialist counsellors were located within the organisation's Occupational Health Service. In order to evaluate the impact of the counselling service, sickness absence records were examined for each employee for the six months before their first interview with a counsellor and for the six months following cessation of counselling sessions. Clients also completed a number of self-report questionnaires at their first interview and after treatment was completed. A total of 78 clients completed the questionnaires pre- and post-counselling. The results showed that there were significant improvements in psychological functioning following counselling: the clients were less anxious and depressed and their self-esteem had increased. When the mean number of absence events and days lost through sickness was examined, it was found that there was a significant decrease in absences in the six months following counselling compared to the six months immediately preceding the start of counselling. However, scores on the measure of "organisational commitment" were found to decrease significantly after counselling. The authors attempt to explain this finding as perhaps arising from an initial "over-commitment" which itself was responsible for psychological difficulties. However, details of their measure of commitment are not provided so it is difficult to know what to make of this finding.

The only available published evaluation of professional counselling within a British police force was conducted by Powell, Edelmann, Campbell and Thrush (1992). The authors surveyed the first 100 referrals to the force counselling service and also examined therapists' ratings of clients. The majority of clients were males in the 36–45 years age band and 80% presented stress- and/or anxiety-related problems. Most clients (71%) needed four or fewer appointments, permission being needed from the force concerned for any further appointments. Both therapists and clients agreed that 84% of clients benefited from the service and 36% of clients said that the service helped them stay in the force. On the whole clients were satisfied with the service and there was consensus that there was a need for such a service.

The Los Angeles Police Department was amongst one of the first to offer comprehensive counselling and therapy for officers. An evaluation of users of the service during 1973–1974 was conducted by Reiser (1982). He approached 300 officers who had received counselling to determine their satisfaction with the help that they had been given. In addition 39 officers were followed up in order to assess their pre- and post-counselling performance from their personal records and supervisor ratings. Since there was only a 25% return rate to the questionnaires sent to officers the satisfaction data must be treated with caution. Two-thirds of those responding said that they found both the counsellors and the counselling were satisfactory or very satisfactory. There were no appreciable differences in the behavioural measures that were obtainable from officers' personal files prior to or after the counselling sessions although, in all cases, the supervisor ratings indicated an improvement. The attempts to measure more specific cost benefits of the service were not reported. The inconclusiveness of this study's findings demonstrates the difficulties in obtaining clear and unambiguous multi-modal measures of counselling interventions.

With all of these individually focused programmes, be they peer support or professional counselling, the emphasis is primarily on helping the employee to cope with the work-related stressors rather than tackling the stressors themselves. The issues involved in reducing sources of stressors are addressed in the following chapters.

PROFESSIONALISM AND ACCREDITATION IN COUNSELLING

One of the difficulties facing any employer who is considering offering a professional counselling service is deciding who should provide such a service. The field of counselling and psychological therapy is not well charted, and it is very difficult for the uninitiated to assess what particular qualifications mean and what the skills of a particular professional group are. The British Psychological Society has recently instituted a Register of Chartered Psychologists in the United Kingdom. One of the aims of this Register is to provide the public with a list of psychologists who are recognised by the British Psychological Society as having the necessary qualifications and experience to practise independently. The British Association of Counselling also accredits individuals who have undertaken training in counselling skills.

OCCUPATIONAL HEALTH UNITS

A number of forces have responded to the problem of stress by establishing a force Occupational Health Unit (OHU). Occupational health encompasses all aspects of the interaction between health and employment and these units are therefore concerned both with the individual's fitness to do his or her job and the effects of employment on the health and welfare of the individual. In a few British police forces Occupational Health Units, comprising a full-time occupational health physician and support staff, have been set up to cater for force needs. For example, the West Yorkshire Unit has three sections: psychology, welfare and medical. The psychology section handles the confidential counselling scheme and referral system, counselling training for senior officers and psychometric testing of recruits. It also functions as a central facility giving psychological advice and providing expertise in the areas of promotion, training and police operations. The welfare section looks after loan schemes, visiting the long-term sick and other welfare functions, and the medical section, besides attending to general medical commitments, also provides force-wide advice on medical matters affecting police and civilian officers. Staff comprise a force psychologist, a welfare officer, an assistant welfare officer, a part-time clerical assistant, and a force medical officer assisted by a part-time nursing officer.

The Royal Canadian Mounted Police introduced psychological services in the 1980s for their employees (Loo 1985, 1987). This was a centrally planned initiative which emphasised a preventive approach to mental health and used a number of strategies for promoting and maintaining psychological health. These included:

(i)   use of psychological procedures for recruitment and selection;
(ii)   education about mental health incorporated into training of recruits and officers;
(iii) regular medical examinations and checks;
(iv)   psychological assessments both before and after any extremely stressful duties;
(v)   training for supervisors;
(vi)   introduction of an employee assistance programme.

EMPLOYEE ASSISTANCE PROGRAMMES

These programmes were set up in the 1960s and 1970s by companies in North America to offer a quick response counselling and support service for employees and their families (Reichman and Beidel 1989). Employee Assistance Programmes (EAP) have also begun to be introduced into the UK in the last few years. These are systematic attempts to offer help to the employees of an organisation in an accessible and structured fashion.

Moriarty and Field (1990) have suggested that in implementing EAP services in police forces two variations should be made in the usual way of operating. They suggest firstly that EAP services should be offered *before* any adverse reactions in the individual. For example they suggest that during known stressful periods, eg initial entry, the officer should be required to have a "lifestyle assessment". Secondly, they propose that an officer who is deemed to need help should be mandated to attend the appropriate services.

SPECIAL ASSESSMENTS AND FOLLOW-UPS

There may also be a place for special one-off assessments of an individual officer's psychological health. Situations that might require such interventions would be prior to undertaking particularly taxing special assignments or to being assigned to undercover work. These could take the form of actually selecting particular individuals based on an assessment of their psychological strengths or else might be some kind of psychological preparation or "stress inoculation".

Follow-up work might also be undertaken with these same individuals and with those who have been exposed either to single traumatic events or to the effects of a disaster. It is not suggested that all officers so involved necessarily require psychological assistance but they may well need an opportunity for debriefing and for exchange of information and feelings among their colleagues in order to allow some emotional release.

Mitchell and Bray (1990) have described a systematic approach to debriefing following traumatic incidents involving a number of officers which they term "Critical Incident Stress Debriefing" (CISD). This relies on having a trained and primed CISD team comprising both mental health professionals and what they call "peer support personnel". These peer personnel are drawn from the emergency services. The actual debriefing is carried out by a team of about four people drawn from the wider CISD team. The debriefings are conducted through group meetings: "The two major goals of debriefings are to reduce the impact of a critical event and to accelerate the normal recovery of normal people who are suffering through normal but painful reactions to abnormal events." These goals are tackled via some educational/information input and by using a variety of strategies to encourage identification of feelings about the event and ventilation of those feelings. Mitchell and Bray (1990) recommend that such debriefings are held sometime between 24 hours and 72 hours after the incident. Participants are given follow-up telephone numbers for use if they require any further help.

For individual officers who are involved in traumatic incidents it may be useful to have a policy of mandatory counselling. This would overcome the institutional problems and the potential stigma attached to the use of counselling services. The New Zealand police force have defined when mandatory referrals will be required for officers. Referrals are compulsory after the following types of incidents: any use of deadly force; accidental deaths of officers; accidental death or serious injury of the public caused by officers; injury or threat to the life of officers; disaster victim identification work; multiple deaths; multiple and bizarre homicides. Staff who were not directly involved at the scene of the incident but who were themselves affected may also be mandated to attend for counselling.

SUMMARY

There is wide variation within British police forces with respect to the recognition of and priority given to stress-related problems. There are also considerable discrepancies in the resources, both financial and personnel, allocated to remedial interventions. The

preferred styles of intervention have encompassed peer counselling, professional counselling and occupational health schemes.
However, the evaluation of these various strategies is very piecemeal and not always entirely systematic. Evaluation of the cost-
effectiveness of any scheme is rare. Such evaluation is, indeed,
problematic because of difficulties in measuring the desired
outcomes and in estimating real costs and benefits.

There is some suggestive evidence that informal support networks and peer support or counselling can be problematic. Officers may be reluctant to be entirely open with their peers. Officer
counsellors may become burdened by the disclosures of fellow
officers and themselves succumb to stress symptoms. Informal
procedures make discovery of any organisational features
contributing to stress outcomes difficult to discern.

More forces are turning to professional counselling practitioners
to offset some of these potential difficulties. Advice to forces
offering this kind of provision suggests that the introduction of the
service should be accompanied by a written policy statement in
order to create a positive climate in which people are encouraged
to seek help. Credibility, independence and confidentiality are
crucial elements. Ideally the service should be accessible by self-
referral.

More sophisticated or integrated services such as can be provided
by Occupational Health Units or Employee Assistance Programmes
have been introduced by some forces and police departments.
Whilst their introduction may well signal important institutional
messages to the workforce concerning the management's commitment to staff welfare, it is not entirely certain how cost-effective
such arrangements are in practice.

CHAPTER 7

Organisational and Management Aspects

Earlier discussion, in Chapter 2, examined how many of the sources of routine stress within the police related to the style and structures of the organisation and management of forces. Typical stressors include staff shortages, work overload, time pressures and deadlines, poor internal communication, and perceived lack of support from senior staff.

Hayes (1988) describes problems for the police in recruit selection, training, career development and discipline procedures. He concluded: "A good management system should produce officers who are competent professionally, and who receive the necessary support to fulfil their professional function."

However, as the Joint Working Party (1987) points out:

> the provision of a counselling facility does not excuse management from its responsibility for the health, welfare and morale of staff— counselling is not a panacea. It is a possible cure for individuals with anxiety problems. Prevention is always preferable and the main concern of the organisation should be the prevention of casualties caused through unnecessary stress.

Avoidable stressors resulting from poor management, and faulty organisational structures and systems such as distant and autocratic supervisors, absence of positive feedback on performance, apparent arbitrariness of promotion or selection for specialist postings, can result in low morale, increased absenteeism, and high staff turnover. This in turn impacts on the quality of service delivered to the public and potentially impairs police–public relationships (Alkus and Padesky 1981). In a management review of the London Metropolitan Police, it was noted that the force was aware that it would become more difficult to maintain its current establishment in the face of a diminishing number of younger people and that existing officers were already leaving the force to take less demanding jobs (Wolff Olins 1988).

Care for the morale and welfare of officers and civilian members of police forces has led to some fundamental questioning of police personnel practices. Jones (1987b), in an analysis of the role of women in the police, documents that at that time no force in the United Kingdom had an equal opportunities policy available, or guidelines for officers making appointments. The issuing in 1989 of a Home Office circular on Equal Opportunities Policies in the Police Service has drawn attention to the issue of fair treatment of staff (Home Office 1989). In pursuing such policies, the police as a major employing organisation have had to look at their recruitment, selection, promotion, training and deployment practices. Work in the development of job descriptions and skills profiles for posts has been hastened by Industrial Tribunal cases being successfully contested by officers. As argued in Brown, Campbell and Anderson (1990), the need for improved personnel practices has been accentuated by equal opportunities issues, affecting the very nature of the organisation and having an impact on the whole of the workforce.

This chapter will look at the following areas in some detail:

- Personnel practices, ie methods for selecting, promoting, supporting and developing the careers of staff.
- Training, ie of recruits and supervisors.
- Communication, ie examining ways to improve information flow and support between staff and between different levels in the organisation.

IMPROVING PERSONNEL PRACTICES

Professionalising Personnel Departments

Until relatively recently, police forces in the United Kingdom have not employed professionally qualified personnel managers, these functions often being performed by unqualified senior police officers. It is still relatively rare for forces to have civilian staff occupying senior positions within police personnel departments.

A first major impetus towards professionalising personnel departments came with the increase in the employment of civilian staff within British police forces. Following a directive from the Home Office, forces were instructed to make economies and increase efficiency by employing civilian staff to undertake administrative and support functions in order to release police officers for operational duties. As a consequence, about one-third of personnel employed by police forces are civilian staff who have different pay and conditions of service. Some forces have amalgamated their civilian and police personnel departments, whilst others have varying degrees of overlap. Because of this development, police forces have become more exposed to professional personnel practices.

Some forces have begun to use a variety of psychological services including methods of personnel recruitment and selection. Rodie and McGurk (1989) have described the contributions being made by occupational psychologists in a number of areas. These include the selection of civilian custody officers; the design of assessments for police staff; the development of annual performance appraisal schemes; the application of ability tests to select computer operators.

Equal Opportunities Issues

The recent drive towards equal opportunities employment practices has focused further attention on the need for this specialist personnel knowledge.

The Home Office Circular 87/1989 recognises that treatment which is unfair or unlawfully discriminatory can lead to resentment on the part of those who suffer such treatment. It also acknowledges that some groups, notably women and ethnic minorities, may be particularly susceptible to unfair treatment. The circular commends the institution of equal opportunities employment practices in order to benefit all the workforce such that the best qualified are selected for promotion and/or specialist postings, a move that in turn facilitates efficient and effective service for the public. Implementation of good personnel practices involves fairer and more objective procedures for recruitment, promotion and selection. These in turn rely on effective job descriptions and adequate skills profiles for posts; supportive and meaningful appraisal systems; positive career development and fair appointment procedures; and appropriate grievance procedures to arbitrate in the case of complaints.

In a survey of the North Wales Police conducted by Baker and Waddon (1991) it was instructive that women officers perceived that force to be less effective in terms of its equal opportunities policies for women than was the case within the police generally. They also believed that there were more obstacles to their promotion than existed within other groups. Gender issues in the police service are more fully explored in Chapter 5.

In February 1990, the Police Training Council set up a working group to examine issues related to career development systems. The results of their deliberations were reported in Home Office Circular 104/1991. A key element in this paper is the commitment to equal opportunities. A fair, open and objective approach, which the circular recommends, should include the publication of job descriptions, criteria for promotion, and feedback for officers on their performance. Of paramount importance to open and fair promotion and selection is an effective staff appraisal system. The circular states that a good staff appraisal system "should benefit not only individual officers but the police service and the community as a whole, since it clearly is in the interest of all for the skills and aptitudes of every police officer to be recognised and used effectively".

Equal opportunities policies should have an impact on a more equitable access to specialist postings. A number of commentators have suggested that a prevailing view among police officers is that women's failure to enter the full range of police specialism is due to lack of career ambition. However, this is not supported by the research findings (Jones 1986; Coffey, Brown and Savage 1992). Coffey, Brown and Savage (1992) show that women officers have similar career aspirations to those that are reported for men (Smith 1983) but are deflected from applying for promotion because they believe their applications will be blocked by senior managers or that they will fail to be selected.

Career Breaks

Woolfenden (1989,1991) reports the problems faced by women officers with children who wish to resume their police careers after maternity leave. Of particular note is the number of women who retire on medical grounds within two years of resuming work after maternity leave. Woolfenden has noted the importance of childcare facilities and working arrangements for this group of officers.

In a major study of policewomen returning after maternity leave, Fletcher (1990) discussed this at some length. A questionnaire survey was sent to 192 women leavers, 207 presently serving women officers, and 110 presently serving policemen. The study revealed a high level of interest from women officers in the resumption of their careers after a maternity break.

Fletcher proposed a package of measures to facilitate women's return to policework. This involves keeping in touch with the officer during her break from work, retraining or refresher courses, and flexible working arrangements such as job sharing or part-time working. Fletcher points out that such arrangements could apply equally to men via career breaks which could provide male officers with a short-term "sabbatical" from their career. Such arrangements may well alleviate pressures on the stressed officer, as well as making return to work easier for women after maternity breaks. Women also would be entitled to take non-maternity career breaks. Following adjustments to Police Regulations to allow variations in working patterns, six British forces agreed to participate in a trial of part-time working. The results of this have not yet been reported.

Appraisal Systems

Staff appraisal systems may result in discomfort or resentment both for the appraiser and for the person being appraised. Within the police, as in other organisations, appraisals contribute to eligibility for promotion or specialist appointments. Being underpromoted or not working within a preferred specialism are sources of stress within the police (Brown and Campbell 1990), and may especially affect women and ethnic minorities. Jones (1986) describes attitudinal prejudices operating against women officers within the police which are documented more fully in Chapter 5.

Walklate (1992) undertook a content analysis of references given for 153 of the 679 successful applicants (22%) to a southern British police force during 1984 to 1987. The references provided for candidates were completed on a standardised form which asked questions about the truthfulness, honesty and sobriety of the candidate, the suitability and qualities of the person, and gave space to provide any other observations which might assist in the decision to appoint the individual. Most referees were middle-class males, teachers, company directors, members of the services or doctors. The quality most often mentioned for men was level headedness (81% compared with 19% of mentions for female applicants). Intelligence and sense of humour were qualities given only in references for male applicants whilst good moral values, dedication and reliability were qualities mentioned in women candidates' references only and were not evident at all in men's references. Athletic ability was the most often mentioned quality for women candidates (53% compared with 47% for men). Women referees tended to use different qualities from male referees and women more often supported women's applications. Walklate (1992) concluded that women challenge the identity of the police and it is striking that their moral worth features as a significant qualification for their recruitment into the service. Policewomen, Walklate argues, are "anomalous": "They potentially disrupt a taken for granted order in which the regime of rationality designed by men, for men, and understood by men, is threatened."

Richards (1987) draws attention to gender-specific meanings of attributes when applied to men and women in the academic world and the impact that these have. It is argued that discriminatory language is employed either unthinkingly or unwittingly to favour men and undermine women—thus she's bossy but he's decisive, she's curt but he's incisive, she's aggressive while he's competitive. Richards suggests that ultimately this discredits appraisal systems and will be detrimental to all, not just to specific groups.

The London Metropolitan Police introduced a new annual performance appraisal in an attempt to overcome criticisms of their previous method of assessing the performance of officers (Wareing and Morgan 1988). Applying a methodology devised from Kelly's Personal Construct Theory, consensually agreed criteria were identified for inclusion in the new appraisal procedures. Appraisal and promotion assessment were separated into two distinct functions. In addition, supervisory officers were trained to carry out these functions. Wareing and Morgan (1988) reported favourable reactions from both appraisees and appraisers in a pilot run of these procedures.

Assessment Centres and Psychometric Testing

Police selection and promotion procedures in both the United States and Australia have for some years made use of personality and aptitude testing as part of their armoury of selection techniques (Dunnette and Motowidlo 1976).

Adler (1990) reviewed the impact of assessment centres on the promotion process for women officers in United States police departments. Amongst agencies using an assessment centre, the percentage of eligible women promoted to sergeant was 12.2% compared to 4.8% using traditional promotion systems. The assessment centres make use of scores from a written promotion examination which, as a consequence of various legal challenges, has been thoroughly revised to eliminate cultural bias. In the Detroit Police for example, final rankings on promotion lists are based on a combined rating comprising 65% written examination score; 15% performance evaluation; 10% promotion board evaluation; 6% seniority; 2% veteran status; 2% college credits.

In the New York and Washington police forces, seniority is no longer considered as a criterion for promotion. In the latter police force, position on the promotion list is entirely determined by written examination and assessment centre scores.

Adler (1990) reports that from limited research, the outcome of these procedures has had a marked impact on the morale of officers who perceived they had lost promotion opportunities, with the greatest feelings of resentment and frustration amongst white officers, both men and women. Few forces in the United

Kingdom use assessment centres so little is known about their impact. Only one model of an assessment centre has been subjected to formal evaluation. Feltham (1988) reported on the validity of assessment centres used to choose serving police officers for places on a national accelerated promotion scheme run by the United Kingdom Home Office. Described as extended interviews, these have been used since 1962 for selection to the police "special course", an accelerated promotion programme open to constables. The format of extended interviews consisted of group discussion; a committee exercise; a written appreciation; a drafting test; cognitive tests; a battery of tests of verbal and non-verbal reasoning; a general knowledge test; interview by a panel; and peer nominations. Three assessors agreed an overall rating for each candidate. These scores were correlated with training criteria and performance criteria following successful completion of the extended interview. This research indicated that the extended interview procedure overcollected information and that the overall ratings were best at predicting subsequent job performance, but poor at predicting promotion. Feltham concluded that the extended interview technique is performing a worthwhile function, despite the in-built redundancy of information.

There has been a significant growth in the use of assessment products and services for selecting and developing staff across occupational groups (Bartram 1991). In the United States, psychological testing has become a standard part of the selection process for law enforcement officers (Hiatt and Hargrave 1988). The tests are used to predict the likely performance and psychological suitability of candidates. Inwald (1984) notes that whilst psychological testing can be a powerful tool to help in difficult selection decisions, in the United States legal and ethical issues have been raised. It has been suggested that tests may be intrusive and potentially discriminatory and that there is a disagreement amongst professionals about their use.

The American Psychological Association publish standards governing the use of educational and psychological tests and Inwald (1984) discusses how these may be met by law enforcement agencies. Table 25 gives a summary of Inwald's (1984) recommendations about the use of psychological testing.

Table 25. Recommendations for the use of psychological testing in law enforcement agencies

1. Psychological tests should be used with reference to other evidence and test results should not be the sole reason for rejecting a candidate

2. Those responsible for police selection should understand the rationale and basis upon which the tests are founded

3. Qualified persons should conduct the tests, and these should have some guidance and orientation to the particular context of policing

4. Choice of tests should take into account their particular suitability for law enforcement. Tests validated for use on the population at large may not be appropriate to those working in police departments

5. Follow-up interviews should be conducted. These are especially important for those showing significant deviation from test score norms

6. A structured interview format should be followed, thereby minimising opportunities for interview error or bias

7. Jargon should be avoided when providing reports on test scores, and recommendations should be supported by written accounts documenting the rationale and providing evidence for interpretation of test scores

8. Staff responsible for selection should be trained to understand the uses and limitations of tests

9. All testing procedures and results should be carefully documented and regular consultations held between tester and responsible police personnel

Source: Adapted from R. E. Inwald (1984). Pre-employment psychological testing for law enforcement: Ethical and procedural issues. Washington crime news service. *Training Aids Digest, 9,* 1–6.

Mirrlees-Black (1992) has discussed the use of psychometric testing in the selection of firearms officers. She identifies a number of problems associated with this: the predictive validity of personality scores in specific situations; the use of test results with due reference to norms; the influence of contemporaneous factors when taking tests. However, despite these reservations, Mirrlees-Black (1992) concluded that personality tests do provide additional information that may be missed through observation or at interview.

Personality tests can also help to match an individual's prefer-
ences and attitudes to job role while clinical personality tests can
detect possible mental health problems. However, caution is
advised in the application of test results, especially if there is an
absence of a demonstrated relationship between job performance
criteria and employee personality characteristics. If psychometric
tests are to be employed then such preparatory work needs to be
carried out and professionally trained personnel should undertake the testing and the interpretation of the results.

Sickness Monitoring and Absence Management

In Britain it has been estimated that, for 1990, 1.1 million police
working days were lost through sickness at a financial cost of £120
million sterling (House of Commons Home Affairs Committee
1991). The average sickness rate per police officer in 1990 was 11.6
days which adversely compares with other employee absence
rates. Some 25% of absences, it was suggested, were attributed to
stress factors and this in part was due to problems with
management.

The subsequent Home Office Circular (90/1991) made some very
specific recommendations following the Home Affairs Committee's
report: to adopt accurate and standardised methods of accounting
when preparing sickness absence returns; to appoint designated
managers to be responsible for monitoring; and to create a strategy
for managing absence.

Woolfenden (1989) examined sickness absence in a large British
Metropolitan police force, which had been shown to have the
highest annual average rate of days lost due to sickness, injuries
and assaults. In 1989 the average annual financial cost of days lost
to that force was 5½% of the annual police salaries' budget. The per
capita absence rate was 20 days annually. The procedure for
taking sickness absence enabled officers to take up to 7 days
absence from duty without the need for a medical practitioner's
certificate. After the third of such leave periods in 12 months the
individual officer's sickness record was referred to the divisional
commander who could either take no further action, refer the
officer for counselling or advice or withdraw self-certification

privileges. Analysis of the pattern of sickness absences showed that nearly a third of absences were long-term, accounting for 80% of the total days lost. Absence rates were variable across work locations and inversely related to rank. They were highest for women officers with children.

An absence monitoring procedure was then introduced to this force (Crampton 1992) at the same time as the establishment of an in-house Occupational Health Unit. The Unit has responsibility for the central administration of sickness reporting and recording procedures. All absences are recorded on the personnel computer. If the absence is judged to be stress-related, a procedure is followed in which follow-up and liaison are maintained with the Occupational Health Unit. If officers do not resume work after 21 days, whatever the cause of the absence, they are visited by supervisors. Officers may be referred to the Occupational Health Unit if work is not resumed after one month. However, actual improvements on sickness absence rates have not been achieved; in fact the pattern for this force actually showed a small but progressive increase in the per capita rate of sickness absence. Since 1987, when the rate was 18.8%, there has been an incremental increase to the 1991 rate of 23.9% (Anderson 1992; personal communication). Therefore there was no evidence in this force that increased monitoring of absence had any positive effects on overall absence rates.

TRAINING

Recruit Training

There has been considerable work directed at improving the training of recruits, who are amongst the most stressed personnel during their period of probation (Fielding 1987; Brown and Campbell 1990). Earle (1972) conducted an evaluation of two types of training programmes in the United States. Recruits were matched by age, race, education, marital status and previous military history. They were then subjected to two different training regimes. One class received a military training model involving intense physical demands and psychological pressure which included subjecting recruits to verbal abuse. The other class received training that emphasised academic achievement and physical training within a supportive supervisor–trainee relationship. Officers trained by the latter method achieved a higher level of performance goals in the field and reported a higher level of job satisfaction than those subjected to the military model. In another study from the United States, Ruddock (1974) found recruits trained in a "total controlled environment" as opposed to a "guidance approach method" were less successful in developing self-discipline and decision-making abilities.

In the United Kingdom, the London Metropolitan Police in conjunction with researchers (Bull, Horncastle, Jones and Mason 1988) and also the Central Planning Unit (1989) have undertaken research into developing and evaluating police probationer training. The police skills training programme involved role playing exercises, and video feedback to develop interpersonal skills and self-awareness within a supportive teaching framework. An elaborate evaluation of several cohorts of recruits was attempted, including the self-completion of psychometric tests measuring anxiety and self-esteem at strategic intervals over a 60-week period. Unfortunately no control group was included in the evaluation and therefore it was only possible to make comparisons within the group over time. There were also considerable difficulties experienced in the reliable completion of all the research instruments at the appropriate time. Nevertheless the conclusions drawn are of interest in that the training produced positive effects amongst recruits on measures of social avoidance and distress and fear of negative evaluation. The highest impact was achieved during the first 20 weeks. Comments by recruits themselves, who positively valued the training, revealed organisational shortcomings and showed that supervisory pressures had adverse effects on their ability to employ what they had learnt. Potential conflicts between training and practice when probationer officers are located at police stations has been found to be a contributory factor to stress (Bull et al 1988). This study concluded that the compatibility of training objectives and the objectives of the force as a whole is of crucial importance. This study pre-dated the Metropolitan Police's PLUS programme which was designed to achieve the merger of objectives and practice alluded to by Bull and his colleagues. Some further discussion of the PLUS programme is given in Chapter 8.

Thus, despite considerable advances in recruit training there are still potential sources of tension between the philosophies of the trainer and of the operational police officer on the ground. Toch (1973) points out that inconsistency in criteria for evaluating officers' performance (eg operational emphasis on the number of arrests made compared with quality of community service) contributes to low officer morale.

Probationer officers are exposed to a great deal of potential stress during their training which can be offset not only by the new developments in training philosophy and procedures, but also by following these through in practice, which, in some cases, is still not undertaken. Fielding (1987), who undertook a longitudinal study of 125 male and female recruits to a British police force during 1979/80, noted that with the general de-emphasis of formal training and corresponding emphasis on practical experience, the tutor constable occupies a crucial role. Tutor constables instruct probationer or rookie police officers on the skills and techniques of policing on the job and they are often the recruits' first contact with a "street wise" police officer. Fielding points out that much of what the tutor constable has to impart is "subversive" knowledge, ie details of practices for coping with the work which might well diverge from the approved procedure. From Fielding's study it is evident that the initial patrol undertaken by the recruit is stressful. Many suffer "stage fright". Fielding proposes that the new constable should learn the distinction between formal "by the book" procedures and street wisdom. The distinction, Fielding suggests, does not reduce the value placed on formal training by recruits but signals its limitations. Tutor constables are not necessarily better teachers but they are more strategically located.

Training for Supervisors

Management-induced factors have been cited as contributory sources of stress in the police. Studies of a large provincial English police force (Brown and Campbell 1990) and of the Grampian force in Scotland (Alexander et al 1991) both concluded that managerial practices can be potent stressors.

There are external pressures that are likely to increase and change the workloads of police managers. The Audit Commission of England and Wales has suggested greater devolution to local area commanders, incorporating financial and personnel responsibilities within the command function. The Home Office requires the adoption of equal opportunities policies and career development systems. Training for supervisors should be available so that they are able to carry out their existing tasks as well as these new demands. Such management training for supervisors and administrators to improve their financial, operational and interpersonal skills has been discussed for some time. The Police Staff College at Bramshill undertakes a measure of education in this respect. However, inculcation of such skills is neither systematic nor universal.

During the 1980s many police forces in the United Kingdom adopted the Policing by Objectives (PBO) methodology (Weatheritt 1986). This involved a planning cycle in which global mission statements were to be set by senior managers, thereafter to be operationalised by local commanders and subject to evaluation from those in the field responding to the objectives. This approach has largely fallen into disrepute through management failures to operate the full PBO cycle or to subject the procedure to proper evaluation. Lack of appreciation or knowledge of the technique contributed to the demise of PBO which in turn can partly be attributed to non-existent or inadequate training (Weatheritt 1986).

New management initiatives have been stimulated by the Quality of Service declaration (Association of Chief Police Officers 1990). This comprises an ambitious programme incorporating internal quality of service (ie management systems) and external service delivery (ie response to the public). Personnel systems involve properly conducted appraisals, career support, equal opportunities monitoring and grievance procedures. External service delivery is evaluated via performance measurements and attitude surveys. These are new areas of concern, and need to be supported by carefully designed management training if these initiatives are not to founder. If managers are not given the appropriate training for implementing such new initiatives, stress may well be increased rather than decreased overall.

McDonald (1989) notes that the responsibility for staff welfare should not be removed from supervisors and managers and yet few receive any formal training or support in these functions. Improvements at national level and locally designed support programmes may go some way to alleviate the stress amongst service managers in the police, and to mitigate some of the consequences on junior officers of management inadequacies.

COMMUNICATION

Group Processes

Poor communication features in many studies as a reported source of stress in the police service. Various procedures have been suggested to improve the flow of communication between staff at equivalent levels and also between staff of different ranks.

Live-in retreats have been initiated by the New York Police Department (Sandler and Mintz 1974) with claimed success in helping to remove misunderstandings that existed between individuals, and leading to greater commitment to common goals. Gardner (1988) describes a similar programme for the Staffordshire Probation Service. Small groups of workers and support staff meet for three days in a comfortable environment away from the workplace. The retreat enables all grades of staff to discover sources of stress, to share those work situations which create the most disabling stress, and to move toward appropriate coping strategies. Learning to verbalise feelings in appropriate non-threatening ways can help to improve interpersonal relationships and lead to improved problem-sharing in work groups.

Some organisational arrangements promote groups that are unwilling or unable to change because of the protective climate surrounding the maintenance of the status quo. The ethos discourages the airing of minority opinions and the group or organisation becomes more concerned with its own maintenance than with seeking the optimal solutions to problems. In a now classic study Janis (1972) analysed the social psychology of the deliberations of

President Kennedy's administration which led to the Bay of Pigs policy debacle.

Janis' analysis identified a particular type of decision-making labelled "group think" which occurs within highly cohesive organisations. This is characterised by a preoccupation with the party line such that contrary information is distorted or ignored. Janis described typical behaviour patterns that characterise group think: (i) illusion of invulnerability, ie a belief that failure is impossible; (ii) rationalisation, ie the use of a mechanism that distorts the meaning of unwelcome or unpalatable information; (iii) a belief in the superior morality of the top managers or leaders; (iv) stereotyping the views of others; (v) the use of self-censorship to foster the illusion of agreement and unanimity; (vi) conformity pressures which force members of the group or organisation to keep their doubts to themselves; (vii) the suppression of doubt through the self-appointed "mind guards" who also protect the group from exposure to adverse information from outside influences.

Group think is not just a phenomenon of political organisation and can be applied to the police service, in which autocratic leadership is resistant to criticism. Janis suggests that group think can be avoided if the supervisor/leader (i) suspends judgement as long as possible; (ii) encourages criticism; (iii) invites outside expertise; (iv) encourages one or two members to play "the devil's advocate" whose specific role is deliberately to argue against a proposal. Janis also suggests that decisions should be made in stages rather than on a once and for all basis.

The structure of groups has been demonstrated to affect the pattern of communication and the efficacy of the group's performance. Wilke and Van Knippenberg (1988) describe four types of communication networks linking people and positions based on a now classic series of psychological experiments. In these, participants were seated around a table separated by partitions. Slots in the partitions were manipulated by the experimenter to control which of the participants might receive or send pieces of information. Two of the networks are centralised structures, the chain and the wheel, and two are decentralised structures as illustrated in Figure 2.

Centralised structures

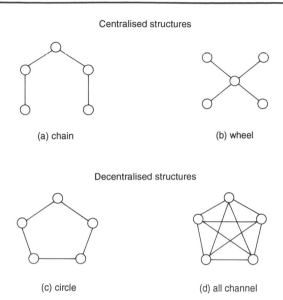

(a) chain   (b) wheel

Decentralised structures

(c) circle   (d) all channel

Figure 2. Communication structures. Source: based on H. J. Leavitt (1951). Some effects of certain communication patterns on group performance. *Journal of Abnormal and Social Psychology*, **46**, 38–50.

The wheel type of arrangement, having a central co-ordinating position, was found to be the most efficient in getting tasks accomplished. This configuration produces a stable organisation and permits straightforward tasks to be completed quickly and accurately. This is representative of a traditional authoritarian type of organisation. The leader is in complete control, members cannot easily communicate with each other, and so the leader has the only access to all the information.

The chain is also an autocratic structure but has two hierarchies. The leader is in the centre and controls the two intermediate leaders, who have no real contact with each other. This pyramidal structure is typical of the police service. The psychological studies, reviewed by Lindgren and Harvey (1981), revealed that this arrangement is stable but has poor capacity to adapt to change and the morale of group members is low.

The decentralised structures are more democratic, and leadership which is based on qualitative factors is more likely to emerge than leadership imposed through the structural position of individuals. The decentralised groups are found to be markedly superior in terms of flexibility and adaptation.

The morale of leaders in the chain or wheel structures was good but the other members of the group were dissatisfied. The morale of the decentralised groups was uniformly high. Later research revealed that centralised structures are more efficient with simpler problems, while the decentralised arrangement is more effective for complex ones.

In centralised groups, the individuals occupying the key position at the centre have a good deal of autonomy and independence. This leaves them free to solve problems quickly and to co-ordinate information. However, the more complex the problems then the greater the amount of information needed, and the key role becomes saturated with data. Coordination becomes more involved and decision-making more difficult. In these situations the morale of the key post holder declines as he or she becomes overloaded, and the proficiency with which the task is performed also declines, leading to a cycle of further demoralisation. Further experiments showed that the performance of the decentralised groups speeded up when positive rewards were introduced to members to encourage efficiency in completing tasks. The centralised groups got no better even with the introduction of rewards.

Morale and task performance are clearly influenced by the quality of communication which in turn is affected by the type of organisational structures. For simple tasks a hierarchical arrangement may be appropriate but at the expense of morale. For more complex tasks, in terms both of morale and of proficiency in performance, decentralised communication networks appear more appropriate.

Reilly and DiAngelo (1990) examine the cultural context of organisations that acts to inhibit their capacity both for good communication and for their ability to change. They argue that barriers to communication are embedded in power, prestige and the status of key individuals in an organisation. Thus barriers may be the deliberate creations of those who wish to preserve their importance and significance. They summarise the needs for good communication within an organisation and these are given in Table 26. They conclude that communication is primarily about a working environment in which there are common concerns, a recognition of the common good, trust and security. Effective communication, they argue, is critical if the organisation is to utilise its financial and human resources effectively.

Table 26.   Structure for effective communication

1. Organisation places emphasis on the importance of services and its people

2. People are defined positively and given respect as significantly contributing to the organisation's success

3. The organisation specifies its major goals which all members support

4. Information is freely shared

5. The organisation provides continuing education for the development of its membership, permitting skill renewal and revitalisation

Source: adapted from B. J. Reilly and J. A. DiAngelo (1990). Communication: A cultural system of meaning and value. *Human Relations*, **43**, 129–140

The outcomes of good communication in the police organisation, according to Souryal (1981), are to maximise interaction amongst staff, to enhance shared understanding of goals, policies and procedures, and to minimise misunderstandings and conflicts. Effective police communication should:

(i)   educate staff regarding the organisation's goals, policy and the standards expected in the performance of duties;
(ii)   solicit new ideas;
(iii)   motivate staff by keeping them informed about the progress of present policies and notified of proposed changes;
(iv)   stimulate feedback from the rank and file;
(v)   facilitate expression of grievances from unhappy staff;
(vi)   unite rank and file behind senior staff.

Police forces are noted for their bureaucratic features typified by a formal hierarchical flow of information and an active subcultural network of informal communication. Souryal (1981) concludes that sensible managers make use of both, being mindful, however, of their respective advantages and disadvantages. On the one hand, formal communication tends to be written, precise, authoritative, traceable and establishes responsibility. It can also be rigid, jargon-ridden, directive rather than explanatory and often underestimates the intelligence of the recipients by focusing on the elementary or trivial. On the other hand, informal communication which tends to be personal, unofficial and verbal, can be less intimidating, invites a two-way exchange and can amplify the meaning of the actions required. Informal communication can also be inaccurate, untraceable and may be emotionally laden or distorting. The use of clear, accessibly written formal communication for official business can be effectively supplemented by informal means to reassure, motivate and unite staff.

Barriers to effective communication can be attributed to poor written or verbal expression by the person transmitting the instructions; to failure of the receiver to listen or understand; to overload, ie too many messages received; to filtering, ie distortions or dilution of the content of the communication as it passes from one organisational level to another; and to simple failure to reach the appropriate destination through the maze of bureaucracy.

Quality Circles

The concept of quality circles was developed by Japanese business and their early use was estimated to have saved $25 billion (Melancon 1985). In the United States, Lockheed and Honeywell experimented with them and by 1981 they were being used by American police departments. Dallas and Orlando police were among the first to use quality circles, which consist of small groups whose task is to identify problems and design solutions to them. An early problem identified by a Dallas Police Department quality circle was the cost of prisoner handling. Security officers were trained to accomplish this task, a move which was estimated to have saved $11 000 to the police. A survey amongst Dallas police officers revealed improved morale and quality of work life as a result of quality circle operation.

Shaw (1989) reviews the use of quality circles within the British police service. Shaw uses the Industrial Society's definition of a quality circle as "a team which meets voluntarily and regularly to identify and solve their own work-related problems. Their proposals are then presented to line management for approval." In summarising the concept, the Society suggests that: (i) the team size should be between four and ten members, one of whom is the leader; (ii) that members are free to join and leave as and when they wish; (iii) that the team meets regularly in order to highlight management support and facilitate effective planning of projects; (iv) that the circle selects its own project; (v) that positive solutions that are systematically analysed and supported by a justification are presented; (vi) that topics are within the circle's own area of expertise; and (vii) that presentations are made to line managers in order to gain approval and authority to implement proposals. Shaw's (1989) analysis suggests that the aims of quality circles are to generate increased officer involvement and participation, to stimulate personal development, and to promote practical solutions. He suggests that there should be a steering group within the police made up of senior managers who set operational guidelines. These include: determining the number of circles, their location and timescale; identifying criteria for the evaluation of a quality circle programme; and developing selection and training for facilitators, leaders and circle members. Shaw notes that the advantages for the police would be to improve the quality of work and morale, increase job satisfaction, and develop team building and management skills.

Within the police, Shaw notes that there is likely to be management resistance and scepticism, a lack of implementation, and resource and time constraints. Whilst identifying the benefits for the police, eg enhanced problem-solving, improved communication and a greater receptivity to change, Shaw offers little empirical evaluation of the outcome of quality circles on the organisation. He notes that some American police departments have used quality circles and that results of these experiments will be published in due course, but little evaluative evidence has been forthcoming.

SUMMARY

Professionalising personnel practices and improving training and communication can provide procedural changes that might help to change the organisational climate. Management style and systems have been much criticised for contributing to officer stress. Better managed systems for monitoring sickness absence, more flexible programmes such as career breaks and more effective communication should help to combat criticisms.

Poor communication and lack of managerial support are frequent criticisms levelled at senior officers in the police service. Understanding some of the psychological processes involved in communication and group dynamics may assist in addressing these problems. Certain communication patterns and group structures are thought to be differentially effective in achieving a range of organisational goals. A more explicit attempt to design appropriate communication systems may help to minimise the impact of a number of organisational and operational stressors.

CHAPTER 8

The Cultural Context

POLICE CULTURE

Analysis of the police culture is necessary not only to understand the concept of stress within the context of policing (Callan 1989), but also in order to effect any significant and enduring remedies to eliminate, or more modestly, to minimise the occurrence of stress casualties. Classically, the concept of culture has been employed by anthropologists in their study of remote peoples. The concept has been adopted by sociologists to examine the values, beliefs and patterns of behaviour within occupational groupings. More recently, industrial and occupational psychologists have undertaken analyses of corporate culture in order to have an impact on successful management and business practices (Payne 1991). Studies have examined the bases for organisational effectiveness and also their responsiveness to change. Payne observes that organisational cultures need time to consolidate values and processes but that without a willingness to adapt the culture could collapse. The state of collapse is manifested by senior people in the organisation being unable or unwilling to see the threats that exist, procedures becoming hidebound and causing resentment, the leaders' goals losing touch with other parts of the organisation. If collapse is to be avoided, says Payne, the culture must change.

Callan (1989), an anthropologist, comments that on reading the literature on occupational stress within the police, it is striking how the term is typically used as an explanation of how or why something went wrong. Stress, as used by the police service, Callan argues, functions as a category of explanation either for an individual's failure, or to offset any claims against the organisation's structures, or as indemnity against corporate failures. This notion of blame or culpability is seen as central to the police culture.

Considerable research effort has been addressed at examining and explicating the concept of police occupational culture. A helpful review of this work is provided by Holdaway (1989) and an earlier edited collection (Holdaway 1979) lays the foundation of much research effort. It is not proposed here to present a detailed treatise on all the various aspects of police occupational culture, but rather to draw upon some recurring themes in order to provide a framework within which to present ideas for change.

Whilst it might be conceded that the police service should not be characterised as having a simple, homogeneous global culture, there are some strong unifying features. As Fielding (1989) has observed: "the occupational culture is actually many subcultures; nuance and colorations arise from regional differences, differences in ambition, divergent perceptions of the police mission, varying experiences of the organisation and so on." Nevertheless the pervasiveness of the domination by white males originating from working-class backgrounds, combined with the strong hierarchical structures, encourages widespread conformity to the organisation and its values.

The research reviewed in this book presents a picture of an organisation whose own structures and style create many of the stress-related problems that adversely affect individuals. In the two immediately preceding chapters, suggestions were made providing remedies for the individual or interventions by management to mitigate the consequences of stress-inducing experiences. In order both to promote the efficacy of these in the short and intermediate terms, and also to engage in a longer term programme of prevention, elements making up the cultural milieu of the police must be open to change. A number of useful ideas have emerged from the literature on police occupational culture, which provide pointers for change.

Social Isolation

Several investigators have explored the sharpness of distinctions drawn between the police world and other domains. Thus,

Holdaway (1989) describes the essential features of police culture as being perceptions of the outside world as a place on the verge of chaos held back only by a police presence. Callan (1989) discusses the boundary sensitivities of the police in wishing to limit knowledge about the organisation and restrict access to outsiders. Punch (1979) draws attention to the lack of police officers' experience in and with other occupational groups and also the segregation, fostered by training regimes, that limits exposure to views or values other than those sanctioned by the police.

Secrecy

Allied to this sense of separation and isolation, is the issue of secrecy. Punch (1979) has discussed peer solidarity that functions to insulate lower ranks both against their superiors and against outsiders. One outcome of this has been a certain defensiveness that has resulted in some resistance to self-scrutiny and to outside research (Weatheritt 1986; Young 1991). Young (1991), Reiner (1991) and Holdaway (1980) all document their difficulties in gaining access to the police in order to undertake their research and also the suspicion that met their field work.

Resistance to Change

Young (1991) and Bradley, Walker and Wilkie (1986) comment on the resistance the police have towards change. The former argues that social changes will occur only when irresistible and more powerful forces are brought to bear from outside. The latter researchers describe this resistance to change as a type of pessimism, eg: "whatever we do, things will not improve, we are prisoners of forces beyond our control". Maintaining the status quo is to a degree a game played between the police and those outside forces, but also within the organisation itself. Change tends to be brought about by external factors such as legislation, procedural requirements as in the Police and Criminal Evidence Act, and recommendations from Commissions of Enquiry (Bradley, Walker and Wilkie 1986).

Informal Practices

Fielding (1989), amongst several research workers, observes the dysfunction between the legal and social realities. This operates at the level of informal practices of short cuts, fiddles and bending of rules which contravene formal procedures. The recruit is especially vulnerable here. A wish to show solidarity to immediate colleagues requires the demonstration of informal rule knowledge, whilst supervisors are looking for evidence of compliance to formally laid down practice and procedures.

Callan (1989) describes how occupational cultures construct their own moral theories. These may be based on commonsense rather than rule book regulation of face to face encounters with the public. Callan points out that this "commonsense" includes social assumptions that may not be universally accepted by the public. Indeed, such assumptions may possibly create unease with particular sections of the public.

Paperwork especially is seen as irksome by police officers and doing paperwork is cited as a source of stress. Holdaway (1989) discusses Manning's and Chatterton's work that revealed the paradoxes built into paperwork. Paperwork is denigrated as it represents some remove from action. It is, however, a method for exerting control and accountability. Techniques for completing "good" paperwork relate to covering your back effectively because this represents officers' accountability to others for their actions. Complaints about paperwork are as much complaints about accountability as about tedium. Manning and Chatterton described police officers who developed their own accountabilities and definitions of police work which, often, were in conflict with notions of policing operating within the rule of law and of that advocated by senior ranks.

Professionalism

Another notion pervading much of the police occupational culture research is that of professionalism. Holdaway (1980) suggests that the concept of a professional police manager emerged during the 1960s and 1970s in Britain as a response to the perceived erosion of the status of senior officers. The advent of technology, notably computers, has helped to foster the proliferation of specialised expertise.

Bradley, Walker and Wilkie (1986) suggest that the issue of professional management has been very much neglected by the police. They describe the police as "reluctant managers" who are often left to their own devices to acquire knowledge and expertise to take on a command management role.

Cult of Masculinity

Fielding (1987) describes this as it relates to policing in the following terms. Policemen are confronted with two mythic images. One is of a police force as a crime- and disorder-controlling, mission-orientated, dispassionate and tough body of men. The other is of women who are weak, emotional, sympathetic and service-orientated.

Jermier, Gaines and McIntosh (1989) have explored the investment that policemen place in the physical danger aspects of policing. This predominantly defines policemen's self-image and lifestyle. Their assessment concluded that as much as actual danger, it is the apprehension of danger that is critical. In actual terms, they demonstrate that whilst policing is dangerous, it is not as dangerous as other occupations such as logging, mining, iron and steel manufacturing and working on the railways. Rather, it is the social construction of policing as crime fighting, involvement in disaster work and human tragedy that infuses the imagery of dangerousness and emphasises the need for physical strength. It is because the physical nature of the work is emphasised, and because policemen enjoy an enhanced solidarity created by external dangers that the entry of women threatens to disrupt these prevalent norms and dismantle group solidarity (Martin 1979). Martin (1989) concludes that policemen's sexism and opposition to women officers is crucial in the maintenance of their own occupational identities.

The results of a participant observation study conducted on the Metropolitan Police have been reported by Smith and Gray (1985). They observe that the prevailing norms in this police force are similar to those that develop in any male-dominated group, especially needs for loyalty and solidarity. They suggest that certain themes get exaggerated, such as male dominance, the denigration of women and the glamour (but not the reality) of violence. They go on to argue that much routine patrolling is boring, uneventful and rather aimless. Much police behaviour can be accounted for by the search for interest, excitement and sensation. Jermier, Gaines and McIntosh (1989) found that dangerous tasks were associated with excitement and occupational gratification. This was more likely to be reported by policemen and they suggest that physical danger is infused with status and prestige that differentiates the salience and value of their role, compared with policewomen. The essence of responding to danger is to keep control. However, as Smith and Gray (1985) point out:

> it is not the true case that the most effective method of keeping control is for the officer to be self-assertive or aggressively dominant. Within the norm of working police officers is the high value placed on dominance and exerting physical control. However, other strategies involving human awareness and social skills are seen to be defusing and more likely women's strategies.

Smith and Gray observed amongst the male subjects of their study that stories of violence and fighting were mixed in with talk about sexual conquests and feats of drinking. Moreover the norm of the talk was to exaggerate the extent and frequency of the exploits.

Sexism

Policewomen enjoyed only a partial role until enabling legislation in Great Britain and the United States legally required equality of access to policing careers. Jones (1986) documents the considerable opposition by both the British Police Federation and the Association of Chief Police Officers to women being included within the scope of the legislation.

Fain and Anderton (1987) have reviewed theories about the differential and subordinate status of women at work. Discrimination against women, it is claimed, serves to preserve male dominance and control. There is certainly ample evidence to show that working women not only occupy subordinate positions within the workforce, but also they tend towards support or service-orientated work (Witherspoon 1989). Berg and Budnick (1986) discuss the notion of gender stereotyping in occupations. This means that masculine jobs are deemed to incorporate high levels of competency, assertiveness, management skills and technological proficiency. Feminine attributes on the other hand incorporate caretaking, emotionality, clerical skills and subservience. When women cross over into masculine jobs they suffer the role conflicts created by the normative occupational characteristics, clashing with stereotype sex role behaviour. Yet it appears that men and women have very similar motives for joining which relate to a public service orientation (Meager and Yentes 1986).

Women, Martin (1989) claims, expose men's emotional masks, inhibit their use of "raunchy" language and offer the potential of sexual intimacy between patrol partners. This fosters competition among male officers, results in threats to the cohesiveness of the group and inhibits talk of sexual exploits. The presence of women also reveals that many routine police duties do not revolve around crime fighting and danger, but involve emotional labour and interpersonal skills. Consequently, policewomen are vulnerable to charges of incompetence and to sexual harassment that disadvantages and undermines them. Part of their occupational life is spent in coping with the tacit or explicit opposition to their presence in the workforce. Sex discrimination excludes them from postings or deployment opportunities and sexual harassment exposes them to sexual jokes, innuendoes, unwanted touching or at worst serious sexual assault.

Martin suggests that men use sexist language to keep women in their place. There are at least two discounting strategies: reference to "ladies" or "girls" focuses attention on officers' gender and implies that they have only ladylike qualities or are immature and not suitable to undertake the full range of tough and dirty jobs. Alternatively, references to "lesbians", "broads", "bitches" or "whores", implies that they have personal or moral failings and therefore are unsuitable as working colleagues. Martin concludes that women are not permitted to be "just officers". Not only are they excluded from career-promoting networks, but also "their interpersonal world often is hassle and their work environment more stressful than that faced by male officers" (Martin 1989).

Poole and Pogrebin (1988) suggest that women lose out either way. Policemen accept incompetent women officers, because it confirms their prejudices, reinforces the stereotype and diminishes the threat. Competent officers may be grudgingly accepted, but are subject to defeminisation through language or ostracism. Faced with this, Poole and Pogrebin argue that women lower their career expectations, develop different working patterns and adjust levels of work motivation. Moreover, Martin concludes that it is the absence of adequate policies to deal with sexual harassment and maternity leave that accounts for the higher rate of premature voluntary retirements of women police officers.

Racism

Holdaway (1991) notes the findings of the Scarman enquiry following the Brixton riots that racial prejudice within the police was probably related to general levels found amongst the British public. It was not until this urban unrest in London that the Home Office and the British police service were prompted to think about ethnic minority recruitment. Holdaway notes that in the United States there have been some fairly dramatic increases in the numbers of ethnic minority officers. Apart from the Netherlands, which has a national plan concerning racial disadvantage, including ethnic minority recruitment into the police, Holdaway shows that European countries have a very low level of activity in this area.

Holdaway's own study of ethnic minority officers in three forces in England found that they experience racial abuse or banter but many are either reluctant to complain or do not regard their experiences as sufficiently serious to warrant a complaint. Moreover, these officers identify the lack of intervention by supervisory officers. In a review of "cop culture" Reiner (1985) discusses racial prejudice in the police service. American sources, Reiner concludes, show that hostility and prejudice towards blacks is a reflection of the racism of American culture generally and especially the social groups from which most police are drawn—lower middle or working class with little more than high school education. Reiner describes similar evidence from many British police studies. However, Reiner draws a distinction between prejudice and discriminatory behaviour and questions the assumption that attitudes held by officers necessarily are translated into hostile actions against ethnic minorities. This distinction was demonstrated in a study of British police officers by Smith and Gibson (1988) who showed that officers' expressed attitudes did differ from their actual behaviour.

STRATEGIES FOR CHANGE

Changing the Social Composition of the Police

Research into the social and economic background of police officers shows that those who join the police service do not constitute a typical cross-section of the population. Punch (1979) writes that "the early police recruiter was advised to go for those of yeoman, artisan stock and to avoid middle class gentlemen". Contemporary police recruiters remain more or less faithful to that advice. Reiner (1979), in a study of police attitudes towards unionism, shows that the majority of police officers, as assessed by father's occupation, come from skilled or semi-skilled manual backgrounds. Educationally, Reiner argues that police are upwardly mobile, with a greater number than expected from that class background attending selective schools. However, Reiner states, whilst educationally the police are upwardly mobile, in terms of the schools they attend, they are not academic high flyers.

There is little evidence that the social class composition of the police has radically changed or that the entry of a variety of socio-economic groupings has impacted the police structure.

Increasing the Number of Graduates

Given the aspirations of the police service towards professionalism (Holdaway 1980) and improved management (Bradley, Walker and Wilkie 1986) efforts made to improve the knowledge base and skill pool included the recruitment of graduates. During the 1960s, the police launched an active campaign to attract graduates and better educated recruits into the service (Hill and Smithers 1991). The Graduate Entry Scheme (GES) was developed subsequent to the Royal Commission of 1960–1962 on the police. This targeted graduates via advertising and offered promotion incentives. The graduate intake increased from 168 in 1968 to 6625 in 1988, although more graduates entered the service normally than came through the GES. Increases in graduate recruitment are claimed to relate to the recession, rising graduate unemployment, increased graduate output, and improved police salaries. However, Hill and Smithers (1991) say that since 1983, the educational level achieved by police recruits has actually declined.

Silvester (1989) undertook a detailed study of graduate recruits who he noted made up 5% of the United Kingdom police workforce at that time. Whilst the flow of graduates through recruitment was around 10% of total intake, Silvester examined the reasons why these individuals prematurely resigned from the police at twice the rate of non-graduate entrants. Half of the graduate leavers did so before completing their two-year probationary period and only about 14% of graduate leavers completed five years service or more. Over half the graduates in Silvester's study indicated that they left because of perceived poor management in the police (compared with 33% of non-graduates who indicated this as a reason for resigning). Most graduates (59%) left because they believed their career prospects to be poor. Whilst senior officers in the study recognised the value of having graduates in the police, interviews with graduate leavers revealed attitudinal problems and resentment amongst their fellow officers and immediate supervisors. Hill and Smithers (1991) in their review of the Graduate Entry Scheme report that it has operated at a low level of efficiency. There has been a high wastage rate and officers have not progressed as quickly as the service would have expected. Evidence from reasons given for resignation would tend to support the suggestion that the graduate entrants tend to succumb to adverse attitudes and management practices rather than managing to influence them.

In the late 1960s the President's Commission on Law Enforcement and Administration of Justice expressed the belief that a college education would provide substantive knowledge and interpersonal skills that would significantly enhance the quality of service provided by police officers (Carter and Sapp 1992). As a byproduct of the Commission's deliberation the Law Enforcement Education Program was created. This programme aimed to encourage police officers to attend college. The argument underpinning the programme was that as college-educated officers rose into police leadership roles they would explore new approaches to policing with greater creativity and better management skills.

Carter and Sapp (1992) reviewed the findings of the Police Executive Research Forum study on police education. The study surveyed approximately 250 000 officers, and demonstrated a steady growth in the educational level of officers. In 1960, 80% had no college-level education; a proportion which had dropped to 35% by 1988. The research showed that college-educated officers were less authoritarian and less cynical. With increasing emphasis on community policing, college-educated officers seemed particularly suited to these assignments because they tended to be better communicators and more effective decision-makers. The research study also noted that women officers tended to have, on average, a year more of college education than their male counterparts. There was no evidence presented to demonstrate that the entry of college-educated officers into the higher echelons of police departments in the United States had any impact on the quality of leadership and management of the service.

Reiner (1991) discusses the issue of educational level in his study of 40 British chief constables. Reiner comments that 80% of chief constables left school at 17 years old, indicating that they had not entered tertiary education at that time. However, Reiner suggests that the norm is moving towards chief constables having degrees. Since the publication of Reiner's study most chief officers who have been appointed have held degrees. There is little direct empirical evidence available that demonstrates the impact that this has had on the quality of management of policing in Britain. However, Reiner does discern an attitude and style shift. Describing various types of chief officer, Reiner proposed that "the boss" represents an ideal type of the early vintage authoritarian officer who is now on the decline. The "bureaucrat" is the very model of a modern chief constable who is sympathetic to professional management approaches, involving consultation but with decision-making underpinned by professional and legal criteria. The "bureaucrat" believes the old tough methods of policing a complex multi-racial society can no longer work. However, it is still too soon to determine the full impact on police officers' attitudes and approaches made by this new style chief officer as the majority in the post still have a traditionalist orientation.

Increasing the Number of Women Officers

At present the police service in Britain has about 11% women in the police officer workforce. A number of commentators argue that increasing the numbers of women officers will constitutionally alter the culture of the police service for the better. Thus Sheerman (1991) suggests that the strengths and character of women will modify the police culture in the United Kingdom. Brown and Campbell (1991) report the results of various attitude surveys conducted in the United Kingdom which indicate that an increasing proportion of women officers want to take part in the full range of policing duties, but that policemen's views still lag behind those of women themselves and also those of the general public. In a recent public attitude survey conducted on behalf of one British police force (Harris Research Centre 1992), two-thirds of those questioned thought it important or very important to recruit more women into the police service. Sokoloff, Raffel-Price and Kuleshnyk (1992) report a similar picture in the United States. Baker and Waddon (1991) in their survey of the attitudes of the members of North Wales Police Force indicate that 24% felt increasing the number of women officers to be a very high priority and a further 28% considered it to be a high priority. However, when these two response categories were combined, increasing the numbers of women came lowest in a listing of 12 priorities for the future development of the force. Increasing the numbers of, presumably male, officers, foot patrols and computers came first, second and third respectively.

An interesting study by Steel and Lovrich (1987) investigated the consequences on police performance of affirmative action programmes in the United States. They summarise the cases for and against affirmative action. Advocates argue that affirmative action is a "rightful corrective of past and existing inequities" whilst opponents castigate such programmes on the grounds of them being "reverse discrimination". With respect to women in public service, the hiring and promoting of the disadvantaged over the maximally qualified, say the opponents, will result in a lower quality, and diminished prestige of services. The proponents on the other hand say that women are neither biologically nor socially so ill-equipped as not to be able to perform traditionally public sector jobs such as fire fighting, school superintending or policing. Rather, women do have the physical and mental capacities to accomplish any task required of them, and the amalgam of men's and women's complementary traits can produce a stronger foundation for service than an exclusively male-dominated workforce. Steel and Lovrich (1987) analysed data collected for a national survey to estimate the degree of commitment to female recruitment amongst police departments. Across the country a top priority to this was assigned by between 17 and 21% of police chiefs. A number of performance measures, including incidence of crime and arrest rates, were examined in relation to departments having higher and lower proportions of female police employees. The researchers concluded that rates of female employment made no difference. In other words service neither deteriorated nor was substantially improved. They note, however, that in view of the fact that those police departments with the lowest levels of female officer utilisation are the most likely to have assigned them "safe" roles, the lack of negative consequence is particularly interesting. The absence of deleterious effects was taken as furnishing support for the presence of women officers in greater numbers, rather than restricting their presence. It still remains to be seen if the impact of women officers' presence at all levels within the organisation has an influential effect. Lunneborg (1989) proposes that the impact of women will not be discernible until a critical mass of 40% is reached within the police service.

Changing the Ethnic Composition of Police Forces

As has been discussed in Chapter 3, the numbers of ethnic minority officers present in UK police forces are relatively low and do not reach representative proportions equivalent to their presence in the population at large.

In the UK, research has been addressed at the issue of the recruitment of ethnic minority officers. Holdaway's (1991) study into
ethnic minority recruitment has already been mentioned. It is
suggested that a strategy to improve the recruitment and retention
of ethnic minority officers is crucial. The benefits of having a multi-
racial workforce to police a multi-racial society are rather taken for
granted. This research, summarised in the Home Office Circular
33/1990 (Home Office 1990a), says that race relations within the
police workforce present problems requiring immediate attention. The senior officers interviewed for the study did recognise
the need to recruit a multi-racial workforce but tended to under-
estimate the extent to which this presented considerable managerial problems.

The evidence available of the impact of ethnic minority officers on
the police operational culture is limited. Holdaway (1991), in
reviewing the American research literature, suggests that whilst
the racial banter may decrease in the presence of large numbers of
black officers, there is no evidence to show that these officers
behave any differently from their white colleagues.

Increasing the Number of Civilian Staff

In the only relevant British study addressing the issue of the
impact of civilianisation, Baker and Waddon (1991) had an indirect measure of attitudes through newspaper readership. The
police officers were marginally more likely to read conservative
tabloids and the civilians more likely to read the *Daily Mirror*, one
of the few left-of-centre tabloids. The civilians in this survey were
more likely than the police officers to think that women, homosexuals, black people or juveniles were treated unfairly by the
police. However, whilst there may be some differences in attitudinal profiles, there was little available evidence to show any impact
of change in police officers' views.

Direct Officer Entry

There is a body of thought which contends that the efficiency and
effectiveness of police management would be improved by

recruiting those with relevant experience directly into senior ranks within the police force. In Britain, a direct entry scheme has been proposed but not implemented.

Reiner (1991) discussed the concept of an officer class of direct entrants into the police. Reiner summarises the arguments for and against by suggesting that on the one hand present problems of management experienced by the police can be cured by the transfer of officers' skills from the military. On the other hand this is to oversimplify the problem because it is the constable who delivers the service to the public and this experience should be seen as necessary for promotion through the ranks.

Hill and Smithers (1991) also discuss direct officer entry. They note that, whilst being opposed by the police in the United Kingdom, in practice this occurred up until the end of the Second World War. They counsel that a radical reform such as reintroducing direct entry, if imposed on a reluctant workforce, would have difficulty in establishing itself.

Hill and Smithers (1991) rehearse the arguments in favour of direct entry: a greater pool of people from whom to choose senior staff; the bringing in of new insights and skills. Police resistance is born of the strongly held belief about the uniqueness of the office of constables who have the power to deprive citizens of their liberty and who have considerable discretion to exercise this power. The police culture, as Smith and Gray (1983) observe, informally sanctions evasion of authority or instructions amongst operational officers. The poacher turned gamekeeper argument is advanced that, in order to manage police officers, supervisors must have come up through the ranks. Given the number of ranks an officer must achieve, and the average length of time spent at each rank, then it becomes somewhat specious to suggest that serving two years as a probationer constable twenty years previously necessarily equips a supervisory officer to tap into the prevailing nuances of the canteen culture.

Multi-agency Approaches

Amongst the criticisms levelled at the police have been their lack of openness and their inaccessibility (Young 1991; Holdaway

1980). Growing awareness by the police that they do not have a monopoly as the only agency to deal with the variety of problems has led to the development of multi-agency cooperation. Thus the Home Office promoted a multi-agency response to crime prevention (Home Office Circular 8/1984); the Interdepartmental Racial Attacks Group articulated a multi-agency approach to racial harassment; an experiment in one area of the UK has revealed the effectiveness of joint training for police officers and social workers in handling child sexual abuse cases (Metropolitan Police and Bexley Social Services 1987).

The aims of multi-agency approaches are: to produce more coordinated responses to complex problems; better information sharing; improvements in the responses of individual agencies; and greater reassurance to those who are the subject of the particular problem. However, it has been striking that the direct consequences of exposing police officers to social work or health professions have resulted in shifts in attitudes amongst police participants. Thus Neyroud (1992) reports that the results of interagency cooperation into the problems of racial harassment allowed officers to become aware of alternative approaches and expanded the possibilities for policing.

Fletcher and Newland (1989), in an evaluation of the joint training of social workers and police officers dealing with child sex abuse, found that both agencies developed a better understanding of the goals and techniques of each other's organisations. The police officers in particular took on the values of supportive interventions underpinning much of the social workers' approach.

PLUS: A CASE STUDY

A significant attempt to influence and change police culture has been attempted by the Metropolitan Police. In August 1988, Wolff Olins presented the results of their study into the corporate identity of the Metropolitan Police. The study team interviewed 200 members of the force, and 50 individuals from outside the organisation, examining the police literature and undertaking observations on patrol and in police stations (Wolff Olins 1988).

The report considered that problems for the Metropolitan Police centred on:

- Lack of a common sense of purpose and uncertainty as to its role.
- Divisiveness within the organisation, with the greatest divisions being manifest between its civilian and police personnel.
- Difficulties in management, especially insufficient time in contact with junior staff, in maintaining quality control or in promotion procedures.
- Attitudes of officers both to the public and internally to the systems and procedures.
- Physical presentation by the Metropolitan Police as an organisation. Many police stations have public reception areas which are neglected and run down. This air of shabby confusion is epitomised in the "sellotape culture" in which notices and signs are stuck up at random.

Wolff Olins concluded that these problems required a "profound cultural change which must accompany and reinforce managerial change". As a consequence the Metropolitan Police introduced its PLUS programme. This focused on nine key areas for change and is being supported by a management team headed by an Assistant Commissioner. The key areas include identifying ways of promoting efficient and effective service to the public by identifying a common purpose enabling fair distribution of talent within the organisation, acknowledging good work, improving communications, simplifying paperwork, promoting pride and confidence and measuring performance. Some £10 million have been set aside for seminars and briefing of staff.

Hyder (1991) highlights areas of difficulty in implementation, most notably the proportion of mid-ranking officers who appear to be blocking the programme. Up to a third of these officers were reported as not attending the briefing seminars. This had been explored by Rose (1990), who suggested the PLUS programme had yet to counter a pervasive aspect of police culture—namely "to do your legs". This encapsulates an attitude that for an officer to criticise or step out of line by questioning existing practice would be to ruin that officer's career. In an organisation that sets huge store on loyalty, to blow the whistle on (senior) colleagues is to break an ingrained taboo. Rose concludes that the ideal of an accountable democratically responsive police service is unrealistic without commensurate internal accountability.

There is insufficient evidence at the time of writing to review the significance of PLUS on the Metropolitan Police culture or indeed the impact the programme may have on the police service in the UK. However, it does represent the most ambitious attempt to date to change cultural norms within the police by the organisation itself.

SUMMARY

Considerable research attention has been given to describing the cultural milieu of the police. It has been noted that police occupational culture can be characterised as being socially isolated, embued with secrecy, resistant to change, concerned with its own sense of professionalism, and exhibiting a degree of racism, sexism and homophobia.

Awareness of these aspects of the cultural environment in which officers work helps in understanding what may generate some of the occupational stressors which exist in the police. Recruitment of officers from groups who, by their minority status, do not share the dominant informal values of the majority group, may change the balance and influence norms that govern behaviour. Encouraging greater exposure to other occupational expertise as in multi-agency approaches or, more controversially, direct officer entry, may also contribute a greater variability to the cultural amalgam of the police service.

Attempts to change the social composition of the police service have yielded little direct evidence that the dominant cultural values observed by analysts have resulted in a less stress-inducing management style. Significant experiments such as the Metropolitan Police's PLUS programme are still too new to determine any enduring cultural shift or to demonstrate that a change from a directive authoritarian management to a more facilitative collaborative style materially affects stress levels in the workforce.

However, there is growing recognition that the police culture exerts a powerful influence on the behaviour and attitudes of the workforce and cultural analysis provides important insights into the management of change as well as changes amongst police managers.

CHAPTER 9

Conclusions

There has been an accumulation of research reports, working party deliberations, government papers and media commentary on the issue of police occupational stress, as is evident from the wide diversity of literature reviewed in the preceding chapters. Farmer (1990), in reviewing research into occupational stress amongst police officers, describes three types of studies. The most common are outcome studies which try to show some relationship between the consequences of exposure to stressors and the nature of the work performed. Process studies focus on intraindividual factors such as personality, coping resources or demographic characteristics which are held to increase or decrease a person's proneness or resistance to adverse consequences of stressor exposure. There are also what Farmer (1990) labels intrinsic factors studies. These examine the roles played by individuals within their organisation and also the structures and dynamics of the organisation in relation to the generation of stressors. However, much of this research is problematic when one is trying to draw firm conclusions about the nature and intensity of stressors impinging on the police. This is because a good deal of the published literature about stress in the police is not of a sufficiently high standard.

Academic conventions require that empirical research should be designed rigorously and have appropriate sampling strategies, control or comparison groups, as well as having reliable and valid measurement. Much of the available published material on police stress does not conform to these conventions. Other problems arise because terms in the area of stress research are not always defined clearly or consistently and commentators or investigators take certain assumptions for granted when presenting their interpretations and conclusions from empirical findings. As a consequence, a number of questions were posed in Chapter 1 which underpin the evidence presented in the subsequent chapters. It may be helpful to review these questions in the light of that evidence as presented throughout the book.

IS POLICE WORK INHERENTLY STRESSFUL?

The broad conclusion is that police work is stressful. However, the detailed working out of the answer to this question presents a more complex picture than this bald statement suggests. Firstly, there are a great many factors impinging on the police that present themselves as potential stressors. These may be categorised into organisational features and operational features which are either internal to the police or are more general factors which impinge on many working environments. By and large, features of the organisation, its management style and systems, and the occupational culture have been found to generate stressors. Routine police operational duties are less likely to become potential stressors except for the rarer, more extreme incidents. Such incidents might be shootings or large-scale disasters and be conceptualised as traumatic stress incidents.

The second consideration is that the police workforce is not a single homogeneous entity across which stressors are evenly distributed. Exposure to stressors is a function of a number of personal, biographical and occupational characteristics. Chapter 4 reviewed the emerging evidence about the key variables that differentiate police officers' exposure to stressors. Rank, role, gender, ethnicity and sexual orientation result in some distinctive patterns of stress experiences. Thus the higher the rank of police officers, the more likely they are to be exposed to organisational and management stressors and the less likely to be exposed to front line police operational duties. The probationer police officer is most likely to be exposed to police operational duties, but least likely to experience organisational and management stressors. Differences are also evident in the exposure to stressors and the role of police officers. Thus detectives are less likely than the uniformed patrol officers to face public disorder situations or to experience shift work. Those driving patrol cars or rapid response vehicles are exposed to some different stressors than those that foot patrol officers encounter. Women and ethnic minority officers, as well as facing many of the same stressors as their white male colleagues, also have to deal with problems attached to prejudice and discrimination both from within and outside the police service. Discrimination and prejudice are also experienced by homosexual officers. Harassment emerges as a significant source of stress for minority groups (ie women, ethnic minorities and homosexual officers).

Therefore it does appear that police officers are exposed to certain stressors as an occupational hazard. However, the answer must be qualified in relation to demographic and occupational characteristics, in that some types of officer are more exposed than others.

DO POLICE OFFICERS SUFFER STRESS TO A SIGNIFICANT DEGREE?

The consequences of being exposed to stressors include a variety of psychological and behavioural symptoms. Identifying the intensity and seriousness of these symptoms is difficult, not least because of individual differences in coping resources. Research suggests that a proportion of police personnel do suffer adverse symptoms to the extent that they require professional clinical support. The suicide rates seem to vary by country and particular police forces.

There is some evidence available that premature medical retirements occurring amongst police officers serving in England and Wales disproportionately account for about 60% of all retirements. However, there are difficulties when interpreting such findings because of the use of medical retirements as substitutes for administrative dismissal and the possible abuse of the system by officers themselves.

IS POLICING MORE STRESSFUL THAN OTHER OCCUPATIONS?

Although no definitive comparative study has been carried out, the answer to this question seems to be no. If anything the levels of stress experienced appear to be lower than those met by other occupational groups. When comparing senior British police officers and their equivalents in the private sector, then superintendents and chief superintendents in most respects were less likely to report type A behaviour patterns, and they reported lower levels of pressure associated with their jobs than commercial managers except in one specific regard. Senior police managers indicated higher levels of work pressures associated with the organisational structures and culture than did the private sector managers. Many of the features identified as potential stressors in the police, such as shift work, poor communication, lack of support, arbitrariness of decision-making, occur in other occupations and are not unique to policing.

There is no compelling evidence that police officers are more prone to suffer PTSD than other on-site emergency personnel. However, systematic research addressing this issue is lacking. Some police forces, such as the Royal Ulster Constabulary, report higher suicide rates amongst their officers compared with the general population, but Australian forces such as the New South Wales Police have rates significantly lower than the general population.

SHOULD POLICE OFFICERS RECEIVE SPECIAL ATTENTION WITH RESPECT TO STRESS?

In the interests of individual well-being and the organisational health of the police, efforts to ameliorate and/or eliminate stress should be continued. A range of short-term, intermediate and long-term interventions and strategies have been reviewed. A recurring problem, however, lies with the usefulness and success of these. Little critical assessment has been made of the relative merits of particular techniques and few cost benefit analyses have been conducted of any improvement achieved.

WILL POLICE WORK BE EQUALLY OR MORE STRESSFUL IN THE FUTURE?

The work on futures forecasting in the police predicts an increase in urban unrest and terrorism. The continued social fallout from economic recession and concomitant reductions in social services and health spending are likely to mean increased workloads for the police in relation to the homeless and mentally disturbed. In addition, pressures for internal management rearrangements with devolved financial budgeting, the implementation of equal opportunities policies, and continued progress in information technology are likely both to present the police service with a continuation of existing stressors and to introduce some new sources of stress.

MANAGEMENT INTERVENTIONS

It was suggested in Chapter 6 that three major strategies are available for dealing with the problems of the stressed officer:

- primary prevention, ie to eliminate or reduce sources of stress and/or to select recruits who are relatively stress resistant;
- secondary intervention, ie to mitigate potential consequences of exposure;
- tertiary intervention, ie to provide support for the stressed officer.

These include both management and clinical interventions (cf Farmer 1990). The former represent adjustments to procedures and systems within the police, whilst the latter involve the introduction of programmes either directly or derived from psychological practice.

Tertiary interventions tend to be curative in approach in that a variety of methods and procedures have been proposed to counsel and support officers in difficulties. Farmer (1990) notes the implications for the largely clinical interventions used. He suggests that police personnel at all levels need training to understand the nature of stress and coping behaviours; that there is a need to create specific programmes to deal with line of duty trauma situations; that family involvement activities can be an important source of assistance to officers; that cognitive-behavioural approaches enable officers to anticipate stress situations and plan appropriate responses; that total fitness programmes may enhance the physical and emotional well-being of staff. These efforts are most likely to be directed at individual officers and represent immediate-term strategies.

Secondary interventions tend to be intermediate-term and are related to features of the organisation's procedures and systems. Manolias (1983) focused on the notion of stress-inducing management. Management style, systems and support were held to contribute to the generation of organisational stressors. Recommendations included making improvements to the training of those responsible for recruitment and selection of staff; better human resource management (such as more effective appraisal systems and the introduction of job descriptions and person specifications as a precursor to promotion or appointment to specialist posts); use of confidential counselling; and the development of health promotion programmes. Through various initiatives stimulated by the responsible government departments or the police service itself, described in the preceding chapters, many of the issues have begun to be addressed. Equal opportunities policies have given particular impetus to the delivery of more sensitive personnel services. It is hoped that the establishment of career development departments and the introduction of new appraisal systems will create a more supportive environment for staff. It is not entirely clear at this stage what the impact of these procedures will be in reducing the stressfulness of the police working environment.

Primary prevention is likely to be a longer term strategy which seeks to eliminate or minimise consequences of stress. This latter approach was explored in Chapter 8 and can be related to the occupational culture of the police. The Metropolitan Police's PLUS programme is perhaps one of the most ambitious efforts to change the internal culture. The consultants, Wolff Olins, presented the Metropolitan Police with a model that required the management to become more open, integrated and united in order to improve its service to the public. To achieve this, they argued, needed a redefinition of the cultural values of the police. This initiative has been followed by many police organisations, but again it is still too early to demonstrate particular effects on the stress levels experienced by staff.

Fielding (1989) suggested that the police culture is both resistant to change and resilient in the face of external pressures to change. Jones (1983) commented on the then contemporary crisis within the police service resulting in a loss of public confidence in the proficiency and probity of police officers' behaviour. Despite various attempts to increase police accountability, most notably through the provisions of the Police and Criminal Evidence Act, the Operational Policing Review makes many of the same points drawn by Jones' earlier commentary.

Murphy (1984) reviewed the outcome of stress management interventions and concluded that such techniques can be effective to help workers reduce physiological arousal levels and psychological manifestations of stress.

In addition Murphy identified some of the problems that undermine the potential success or value of stress management interventions:

(i)   they are often designed to teach workers to cope better with stressors rather than to eliminate or reduce sources of stress;
(ii)   the scientific base is often insufficient to establish with any precision, specific job elements and/or work routines which generate adverse reactions;
(iii)   there are logistical and economic problems associated with an organisation's willingness to alter its structures or schedules;
(iv)   organisations may feel that they have met their obligations by simply introducing stress management programmes.

Murphy (1984) suggested that to maximise the effectiveness of such programmes, organisations should ideally:

(i)   establish and evaluate programmes quickly without major disruptions to existing work routines;

(ii)   address individual differences in susceptibility and coping;
(iii) encompass non-work-related stressors;
(iv)   incorporate interventions within existing employee assistance and/or training programmes to be used in conjunction with organisational change or job redesign.

Chapters 6, 7 and 8 present various strategies and some assessment of individual, management and organisation cultural interventions, to eliminate, reduce and/or alleviate stressor exposure and adverse reactions within the police.

Table 27 presents a brief summary of the types of individual interventions and some comment on the availability of evidence assessing the impact of these. The major dimension distinguishing the self-help remedies and professional counselling is cost. Whilst informal systems may be relatively inexpensive to put in place and indicate that some recognition has been conceded to the problems of workplace stress, they have two major disadvantages. Firstly, these programmes do not address the source of the stress problems, and the help rendered may simply be a palliative that serves to patch people up and return them to the situation causing the problem in the first place. In other words there is a high probability of a recurrence of the problem either with the same or other individuals. Secondly, there are practical and ethical problems associated with confidentiality and the sustainability of these programmes, reliant as they are on volunteer effort.

Professional counselling is likely to cost more in the short term but the advantages lie in having professionally qualified practitioners who offer facilities beyond the training of the volunteer counsellors, and physical environments more conducive to counselling than police force premises.

Second-level interventions aim to impact the structures, systems and procedures of the organisation in an attempt to alleviate sources of stress. Table 28 summarises these. For the most part, their incorporation within the police service has been relatively new and sufficient evidence is not available on the long-term effects to reduce stress.

Table 27. Examples of tertiary interventions at the level of the individual officer

Interventions	Mechanism	Pros	Cons
Self-help	Books, manuals, audio tapes, video tapes	Little or no organisational cost	Little evidence available on effectiveness of change or sustainability of gains
Informal support	Self help groups, colleague support, spouse support	Little or no organisational cost	Little evidence available on effectiveness of change or sustainability of gains
Peer counselling	Self-taught, minimally trained volunteers	Relatively cheap, visible management intervention, in-house understanding of issues	Difficulties in preserving true "peer" relationships, limits to confidentiality, beyond skills of counsellors, availability of appropriate physical environment
In-house support	Welfare officer, chaplain, force medical officer	Relatively cheap, in-house understanding of problems	Confidentiality compromised as can be construed as instruments of management
Career counselling	Personnel, career counselling	Relatively cheap, in-house understanding of problems	Potential conflict between needs of individual vs organisation, problems of lack of training and lack of confidentiality
Physical fitness	Gyms, jogging, running	Some capital outlay, visible management intervention	Equivocal evidence of effectiveness, problems of sustainability
Professional counselling	Externally appointed consultants	Confidentiality, profession-ally accredited, can deal with serious problems, eg PTSD	More expensive option, problems in choosing appropriate counsellors, availability of feedback to management

Table 28. Examples of secondary interventions at the institutional level

Interventions	Mechanism	Objectives	Comments
Personnel practice	Equal opportunities, appraisal systems, psychometric testing, sickness monitoring	Equitable representation within police and fair access to opportunities, constructive personal development, systematic recruitment and selection, promotion, decision-making, improve absence rates, support for sick officers	Little available evidence for actual effectiveness, subjective evidence for perceived improvements, cost-effectiveness claimed but little evidence available, some improvement on short-term absence
Training	Recruit / officer stress-reduction techniques, management courses self-defence courses	Student-social skills centred training, awareness of sources and consequences of stress, introduction to self-help, awareness of physique requirements in restraint and defence techniques	New recruit training courses less stressful to participate in but do not always counteract occupational socialisation, some subjective evidence for individual improvement, little objective evidence available to demonstrate effectiveness
Flexible working	Career breaks, part-time working	Facilitate mid career development, encourage women returners	Little available evidence as yet available on outcome of present experimental programmes

Table 29. Examples of primary interventions at the institutional level

Interventions	Mechanism	Objectives	Comments
Gender ratio	Increase number of women and their lateral and hierarchical representation	To achieve more balanced representation of women in and throughout force, combat sexism, de-emphasise focus on physical skills in favour of social skills	Slow progress, high attrition rate of women, little evidence of cultural impact, evidence of stress on women officers
Ethnic minority ratio	Increase number of ethnic minority officers and their lateral and hierarchical representation	To achieve more balanced representation of ethnic minorities in and throughout the force, combat racism	Slow progress, greater rate of premature resignations, some evidence of better understanding of race issue, little evidence of cultural impact, evidence of stress on ethnic minority officers
Graduate ratio	Increase number of graduates, facilitate gaining of qualifications by serving officers, improve accelerated promotion	Improve educational level and skill pool, increase professionalism, enhance management capability	Modest progress, greater rate of premature resignations, little evidence of cultural impact, evidence of stress on graduates
Direct officer entry	Recruit from private / public sector into senior positions	Increase skill pool, professionalism and management capability	Not as yet implemented
Civilianisation	Increase number of civilians, improve level of qualifications	Release police officers from mundane, routine work, enhance professional skills, increase number of officers for operational duties	Increased numbers, some release of officers for operational duty, some evidence of increased stress through lack of protected posts for officers, undervaluing of civilian staff

Finally Table 29 summarises a programme for long-term primary interventions. This is by far the most speculative in terms of the evidence available and is offered more by way of discussion than a definitive strategy, since the evidence is limited in terms of achieving significant reduction in the stressfulness of the police working environment.

In conclusion, tackling stress within the police, as with many other organisations, requires: (i) a realistic commitment of adequate funding; (ii) a strategic plan; (iii) preparatory research to establish sources of stress and officers at risk; (iv) a phased approach that deals with assistance for stressed officers in the first instance and thereafter interventions aimed at minimising the adverse consequences of stress; (v) a collective longer term approach to reduce sources of stress; (vi) identification of special needs, eg Post Traumatic Stress Disorder; and (vii) built-in evaluation and assessment.

References

Adler, Z. (1990) Hill Street Clues: The US Police Record on promoting women. *Personnel Management,* August, 28–33.

Ahearn, F. L. (1985) The planning and administration of a mental health response to disaster. In J. Laube and S. A. Murphy (Eds), *Perspectives on Disaster Recovery.* Norwalk: Appleton-Century-Crofts.

Alexander, D. A., Innes, G., Irving, B. L., Sinclair, S. D. and Walker, L. D. (1991) *Health, Stress and Policing.* London: The Police Foundation.

Alexander, D. A. and Wells, A. (1991) Reactions of police officers to body-handling after a major disaster: A before-and-after comparison. *British Journal of Psychiatry,* **159,** 547–555.

Alkus, S. and Padesky, C. (1981) Special problems of police officers: stress related issues and interventions. *Counselling Psychologist,* **11,** 55–64.

Allison, T., Cooper, C. L. and Reynolds, P. (1989) Stress counselling in the workplace. *The Psychologist,* **2,** 384–388.

American Psychiatric Association (1987) *Diagnostic and Statistical Manual of Mental Disorders.* 3rd edn revised (DSM-III-R). Washington, DC: APA.

Anderson, M. (1992) Sickness, injury and assaults 1987–1991. Merseyside Police.

Anderson, R., Brown, J. M. and Campbell, E. A. (1993) *Aspects of sex discrimination in the police service in England and Wales.* London: Home Office Police Research Group.

Anderson, W. and Bauer, B. (1987) Law enforcement officers: The consequences of exposure to violence. *Journal of Counselling and Development,* **65,** 381–384.

Anson, R. H. and Bloom, M. E. (1988) Police stress in an occupational context. *Journal of Police Science and Administration,* **16,** 229–235.

Antony, R. (1991) Homosexuality in the police. MA dissertation, University of Exeter.

Association of Chief Police Officers (1980) Study of civilian staff in the police service, career structures and other contemporary issues. ACPO mimeo.

Association of Chief Police Officers (1984) *Stress in the Police Service.*

London: Home Office Publications.

Association of Chief Police Officers (1990) *Strategic policy document: setting the standards for policing, meeting the community expectations.* London: Metropolitan Police.

Audit Commission (1992) *Fine Lines: Improving the Traffic Warden Service.* London: HMSO.

Baker, C. and Waddon, W. (1991) *It speaks for itself: An independent opinion survey of the members of the North Wales Police Service.* Bangor: North Wales Police publications.

Balkin, J. (1988) Why policemen don't like policewomen. *Journal of Police Science and Administration,* **16,** 29–38.

Bartram, D. (1991) Addressing the abuse of psychological tests. *Personnel Management,* April, 34–39.

Beehr, T. and O'Hara, K. (1987) Methodological designs for the evaluation of occupational stress interventions. In S. V. Kasl and C. L. Cooper (Eds), *Stress and Health: Issues in Research Methodology.* Chichester, UK: Wiley.

Berah, E. F., Jones, H. J. and Valant, P. (1984) The experience of a mental health team involved in the early phase of a disaster. *Australian and New Zealand Journal of Psychiatry,* **18,** 354–358.

Berg, B. L. and Budnick, K. J. (1986) Defeminization of women in law enforcement: A new twist in the traditional police personality. *Journal of Police Science and Administration,* **14,** 314–319.

Beutler, L., Nussbaum, P. D. and Meredith, K. E. (1988) Changing personality patterns of police officers. *Professional Psychology Research and Practice,* **88,** 503–507.

Block, P. and Anderson, D. (1974) *Policewomen on patrol: A final report.* Washington, DC: Police Foundation.

Boyle, J. D. (1987) Post traumatic stress disorder: A law enforcement perspective. *Law and Order,* **35,** 52–55.

Bradford City Council (1985) *Bradford City fire disaster long-term strategy: A discussion document.* June 1985.

Bradley, D., Walker, N. and Wilkie, R. (1986) *Managing the Police: Law Organisation and Democracy.* Brighton, UK: Wheatsheaf.

Brett, E. A. and Ostroff, R. (1985) Imagery and Post-Traumatic Stress Disorder: An overview. *American Journal of Psychiatry,* **142,** 417–424.

Brewer, J. D. with Magee, K. (1991) *Inside the RUC: Routine Policing in a Divided Society.* Oxford: Clarendon Press.

Brom, D. and Kebler, R. J. (1989) Prevention of post-traumatic stress disorder. *Journal of Traumatic Stress,* **2,** 335–351

Brook, R. (1990) *An introduction to disaster theory for social workers.* University of East Anglia, UK: Social Work Monograph No. 85.

Brown, G. W. and Harris, T. (1978) *Social Origins of Depression.* London: Tavistock.

Brown, J. M. (1985) An introduction to the uses of facet theory. In D. Canter (Ed.), *Facet Theory: Approaches to Social Research.* New York: Springer-Verlag.

Brown, J. M. (1989) Evaluation of stress awareness training for Sergeants, Superintendents and Chief Superintendents. Unpublished report, Hampshire Constabulary Research and Development Department.

Brown, J. M. (1992) Occupational stress amongst police officers of superintending rank. Paper presented at the Annual Conference of the Police Superintendents Association of England and Wales, Blackpool, UK, September 21–24.

Brown, J. M. and Campbell, E. A. (1990) Sources of occupational stress in the police. *Work and Stress*, 4, 305–318.

Brown, J. M. and Campbell, E. A. (1991a) Less than equal. *Policing*, 7, 324–333.

Brown, J. M. and Campbell, E. A. (1991b) Stress among emergency services personnel: Progress and problems. *Journal of the Society of Occupational Medicine*, 41, 149–150.

Brown, J. M., Campbell, E. A. and Anderson, R. (1990) More equal than others. *Police*, October, 18.

Brown, J. M., Cooper, C. L. and Dudman, P. (1992) Occupational stress amongst police officers of superintending rank. Report to the Police Superintendents Association of England and Wales.

Brown, J. M. and Forde, P. (1989) Occupational stress among Hampshire Constabulary officers. Unpublished report, Hampshire Constabulary Research and Development Department.

Brown, L. and Willis, A. (1985) Authoritarianism in British Police recruits: Importation, socialization or myth? *Journal of Occupational Psychology*, 58, 97–108.

Bryant, L., Dunkerley, D., and Kelland, G. (1985) One of the boys? *Policing*, 1, 236–244.

Bull, R., Horncastle, P., Jones, C. and Mason, D. (1988) *Metropolitan Police Recruit Training in Policing Skills. Phase 2: An independent evaluation.* London: Metropolitan Police.

Burke, M. (1992) Cop culture and homosexuality. *Police Journal*, LXV, 30–39.

Butcher, J. N. and Dunn, L. A. (1989) Human responses and treatment needs in airline disasters. In R. Gist and B. Lubin (Eds), *Psychosocial Aspects of Disaster*. New York: Wiley.

Cacioppe, R. L. and Mock, P. (1985) *Developing the Police Officer at Work.* Bradford, West Yorkshire: MCB University Press.

Cain, M. (1973) *Society and the Policeman's Role.* London: Routledge & Kegan Paul.

Callan, H. (1989) Cultural factors in occupational stress. In J. M. Brown et al, *Sources of Non-traumatic Stress in the Police Service*. London: Police Requirements Support Unit, Home Office.

Campbell, E. A. and Brown, J. M. (1992) Sexual harassment: Experience and Impact. Paper presented to the Women in Psychology Conference, University of Lancaster, July 10–12.

Carter, D. L. and Sapp, A. D. (1992) College education and policing coming of age. *FBI Law Enforcement Bulletin*, January, 8–14.

Cashmore, E. (1991) Black cops Inc. In E. Cashmore and E. McLaughlin (Eds), *Policing Black People*. London: Routledge.

Central Planning Unit (1989) The new probationer training system and its assessment: A note for tutors, trainers and supervisors. Harrogate, UK: England and Wales Police Forces Central Planning Unit.

Central Statistical Office (1991) *Social Trends*, 21. London: HMSO.

Chadwick, K., Hill, A., Highmore, S., and Brown, J. M. (1989) An evaluation of area control rooms. Winchester, UK: Hampshire Constabulary Research and Development Report 107.

Chandler, E. V. and Jones, C. S. (1979) Cynicism: An inevitability of police work. *Journal of Police Science and Administration*, **7**, 65–68.

Charles, M. (1982) The performance and socialization of female recruits in the Michigan State Police Training Academy. *Journal of Police Science and Administration*, **9**, 209–223.

Charles, M. T, and Parsons, K. (1978) Female performance in the law enforcement function; A review of past research, current issues and future potential. *Law and Order*, **26**, 18–74.

Choposky, J. (1975) Cover story. *The Law Officer*, **8**, 9–11.

Clegg, F. (1988) Disasters: Can psychologists help the survivors? *The Psychologist*, **1**, 134–135.

Cobb, S. and Rose, R. (1973) Hypertension, peptic ulcers and diabetes in air traffic controllers. *Journal of the Australian Medical Association*, **224**, 489–492.

Coffey, S., Brown, J. M. and Savage, S. (1992) Policewomen's career aspirations: Some reflections on the roles and capabilities of British women officers. *Police Studies*, **15**, 13–19.

Cohen, R. E. and Ahearn, F. L. (1980) *Handbook for Mental Health Care of Disaster Victims*. London: Johns Hopkins University Press.

Coleman, A. M. and Gorman, L. P. (1982) Conservatism, dogmatism and authoritarianism. *Sociology*, **16**, 1–11.

Cook, M. (1988) Stress Management. *Management Services*, November, 18–21.

Cooper, C. L. (1986) Job distress: Recent research and the emerging role of the clinical occupational psychologist. *Bulletin of The British Psychological Society*, **39**, 325–331.

Cooper, C. L, Davidson, M. J. and Robinson, P. (1982) Stress in the police service. *Journal of Occupational Medicine*, **24**, 30–36.

Cooper, C. L. and Grimley, P. (1983) Stress among police detectives. *Journal of Occupational Medicine*, **25**, 534–540.

Cooper, C. L. and Marshall, J. (1976) Occupational sources of stress: A review of the literature relating to coronary heart disease and mental ill health. *Journal of Occupational Psychology*, **49**, 22–18.

Cox, T., Boot, N. and Cox, S. (1988) Stress in schools: A problem solving approach. In M. Cole and S. Walker (Eds), *Stress and Teaching*. Milton Keynes: Open University Press.

Cox, T., Boot, N., Cox, S. and Harrison, S. (1988) Stress in schools: An organisational perspective. *Work and Stress*, **2**, 353–363.

Crampton, S. (1992) The Merseyside approach to sickness monitoring. *Home Office Police Requirements Support Unit Bulletin* (January), 82–83.

Cullen, R. (1989) *Organisational health in the police service/shift work and the police.* London: Home Office Science and Technology Group.

Davidson, M. J. (1979) Stress in the police service: A multifaceted model. Unpublished dissertation, University of Queensland.

Davidson, M. J. and Veno, A. (1980) Stress and the policeman. In C. L. Cooper and J. Marshall (Eds), *White Collar and Professional Stress.* Chichester, UK: Wiley.

Davies, W. (1988) How not to get hit. *The Psychologist,* 1, 175–176.

Davis, J. A. (1984) Perspectives of policewomen in Texas and Oklahoma. *Journal of Police Science and Administration,* 12, 395–403.

Davis, R. C. and Friedman, L. N. (1985) The emotional aftermath of crime and violence. In C. R. Figley (Ed.), *Trauma and its Wake.* New York: Brunner/Mazel.

Delprino, R. P. and Bahn, C. (1988) National survey of the extent and nature of psychological services in police departments. *Professional Psychology: Research and Practice,* 19, 421–425.

Doyle, C. (1991) *Police recruitment from ethnic minorities: A strategy.* London: Police Research Group, Home Office.

Duckworth, D. (1986) Psychological problems arising from disaster work. *Stress Medicine,* 2, 315–323.

Duckworth, D. (1987) Post traumatic stress disorder. *Journal of Occupational Medicine,* 24, 30–36.

Duckworth, D. and Charlesworth, A. (1988) The human side of disaster. *Policing,* 4, 194–210.

Duckworth, D. H. (1991a) Facilitating recovery from disaster-work experiences. *British Journal of Guidance and Counselling,* 19, 13–22.

Duckworth, D. H. (1991b) Information requirements for crisis intervention after disaster work. *Stress Medicine,* 7, 19–24.

Dunnette, M. D. and Motowidlo, S. J. (1976) *Police Selection and Career Assessment.* National Institute of Law Enforcement and Criminal Justice.

Dunning, C. and Silva, M. (1980) Disaster-induced trauma in rescue workers. *Victimology: An International Journal,* 5, 287–297.

Durham, T. W, McCammon, S. L. and Allison, F. J. (1985) The psychological impact of disaster on rescue personnel. *Annals of Emergency Medicine,* 14, 664–668.

Earle, H. (1972) *Police Recruit Training Stress vs Non Stress. A Revolution in Law Enforcement Career Programs.* Springfield, Ill.: Charles C. Thomas.

Eaton, W. W., Anthony, J. C., Mandel, W. and Garrison, R. (1990) Occupations and the prevalence of major depressive disorder. *Journal of Occupational Medicine,* 32, 1079–1087.

Eisenberg, T. (1975) Labour management relations and psychological stress: View from the bottom. *The Police Chief,* 42, 54–58.

Ellison, K. W. and Genz, J. L. (1983) *Stress and the Police Officer.* Springfield, Ill.: Charles C. Thomas.

Ely, D. L. and Mostardi, R. A. (1986) The effect of recent life events, stress, life assets, and temperament pattern on cardiovascular risk factors for Akron City Police Officers. *Journal of Human Stress*, **12**, 77–91.

Equal Opportunities Commission (1990) *Managing to Make Progress*. London: Metropolitan Police.

Evans, G. W. and Cohen, S. (1987) Environmental stress. In D. Stokols and I. Altman (Eds), *Handbook of Environmental Psychology*, Vol. I. New York: Wiley.

Fain, T. C. and Anderton, D. L. (1987) Sexual harassment: Organizational context and diffuse status. *Sex Roles*, **5/6**, 291–311.

Farmer, R. E. (1990) Clinical and managerial implications of stress research in the police. *Journal of Police Science and Administration*, **17**, 205–218.

Fell, R. D., Richard, W. C. and Wallace, W. L. (1980) Psychological job stress and the police officer. *Journal of Police Science and Administration*, **8**, 139–144.

Feltham, R. (1988) Validity of a police assessment centre: A 1–19 year follow up. *Journal of Occupational Psychology*, **61**, 129–144.

Fielding, N. (1987) *Joining Forces*. London: Routledge.

Fielding, N. (1989) Police culture and police practice. In M. Weatheritt (Ed.), *Police Research: Some Future Prospects*. Aldershot: Avebury.

Figley, C. (1985, 1986) *Trauma and its Wake*, Vols I and II. New York: Brunner/Mazel.

Fineman, S. (1985) *Social Work Stress and Intervention*. Aldershot: Gower.

Firth, J. and Shapiro, D. A. (1986) An evaluation of psychotherapy for job-related distress. *Journal of Occupational Psychology*, **59**, 111–119.

Fisher, S. and Reason, J. (Ed.) (1988) *Handbook of Life Stress, Cognition and Health*. Chichester, UK: Wiley.

Fletcher, M. (1990) *Police women returners*. London: Police Requirements Support Unit, Home Office.

Fletcher, M. and Newland, C. (1989) Hampshire joint training for child sexual abuse investigation. Joint report. Winchester, UK: Hampshire Constabulary and Hampshire Social Services.

Frederick, C. (Ed.) (1978) *Training Manual for Human Service Workers in Major Disasters*. Rockville, MD: National Institute of Mental Health.

French, J. and Caplan, R. (1972) Organisational stress and individual strain. In A.J. Marrow (Ed.), *The Failure of Success*. New York: Amacon.

Funnelle, R. (1992) Survey of sexual harassment of civilian staff within the Hampshire Constabulary. Unpublished report, Hampshire Constabulary Research and Development Department, Report 126.

Funnelle, R., Brown, J. and Woolfenden, S. (1991) Stress in control rooms, a comparative study of Hampshire and Merseyside Police. Unpublished report, Hampshire Constabulary Research and Development Department, Report 121.

Gardner, D. (1988) A sharing approach to the management of stress. *Social Work Today*, **13**, October, 18–19.

Gash, E. (1992) We are all equal. *Police*, **24**, 16.

Gersons, B. D. (1989) Patterns of PTSD among police officers following shooting incidents: A two-dimensional model and treatment implications. *Journal of Traumatic Stress*, **2**, 247–257.

Glowinkowski, S. P. and Cooper, C. L. (1985) Current issues in organisational stress research. *Bulletin of the British Psychological Society*, **38**, 212–216.

Glowinkowski, S. P. and Nicholson, N. (1984) *The promotion pathology: A study of the British police inspectors*. University of Sheffield: Memo 659 MRC/ESRC SAPD.

Goldberg, D. (1978) *Manual of the General Health Questionnaire*. Windsor: NFER.

Gooch, K. (1991) (E)quality of service? Unpublished paper. Bramshill, UK: Police Staff College.

Green, B. L, Lindy, J. D. and Grace, M. C. (1985) Post-traumatic stress disorder: Towards DSM-IV. *Journal of Nervous and Mental Disease*, **173**, 406–411.

Greller, M. (1982) Police stress. *Police Chief*, **49**, 44–47.

Gresty, B. and McLelland, T. (1989) Beating the John Wayne Syndrome. *Police Review*, 13 January, 72–73.

Grieco, A. (1987) Scope and nature of sexual harassment in nursing. *Journal of Sex Research*, **23**, (2), 261–266.

Gudjonsson, G. H. and Adlam, R. (1983) Personality patterns of British police officers. *Personality and Individual Difference*, **5**, 507–512.

Gudjonsson, G. H. and Adlam, R. (1985) Occupational stressors among British police officers. *Police Journal*, **58**, 73–85.

Gularnick, L. (1963) Mortality by occupation and cause of death among men 20–64 years of age: United States 1950. *Vital Statistics Special Reports* Vol. 53(3). Bethesda, MD: USDHEW.

Gutek, B. A. (1985) *Sex and the Workplace: Impact of Sexual Behaviour and Harassment on Women, Men and the Organisation*. San Francisco: Jossey-Bass.

Gutek, B. A. and Morasch, B. (1982) Sex ratios, sex role spillover and sexual harassment at work *Journal of Social Issues*, **38**, 55–74.

Halford, A. (1987) Until the 12th of never. *Police Review*, 9 October, 2019.

Hardy, L., Parfitt, G. and Baker, S. (1989) Physical fitness and coping with psychological stress, the Surrey project. Unpublished paper, University of Bangor.

Harris Research Centre (1992) *Public attitude survey for Hampshire Constabulary*. Richmond, Surrey: Harris Research Centre.

Hayes, P. (1988) The healthy way ahead. *Police Review*, 22 January, 174–175.

Health Education Authority (1988) *Stress in the public sector, high stress occupations working party*. London: Health Education Authority.

Helzer, J. E., Robins, L. N. and McEvoy, L. (1987) Post traumatic stress disorder in the general population: Findings of the Epidemiologic Catchment Area Survey. *New England Journal of Medicine*, **317**, 1630–1634.

Henderson, G. (Ed.) (1981) *Police Human Relations*. Springfield, Ill: Charles C. Thomas.

Henriques, N. (1988) *Inspirational women: Interviews with 12 women who encourage, enlighten and entertain.* Northamptonshire: Grapevine.

Hewstone, M., Stroebe, W., Codol, J.-P. and Stephenson, G. M. (Eds) (1988) *Introduction to Social Psychology: A European Perspective*. Oxford: Blackwell.

Hiatt, D. and Hargrave, G. E. (1988) Predicting job performance problems with psychological screening. *Journal of Police Science and Administration*, **16**, 2, 122–125.

Highmore, S. (1989) Increasing CID operational availability. Winchester, UK: Hampshire Constabulary Research and Development Department, Report 105.

Highmore, S. (1991) A profile of civilian staff within the Hampshire Constabulary, issues for further research. Winchester, UK: Hampshire Constabulary Research and Development Department, Report 122.

Hill, S. and Smithers, A. (1991) Enough of a good thing. Is there still a real need for the graduate entry scheme? *Policing*, **7**, 297–323.

Hillas, S. and Cox, T. (1986) *Post traumatic stress disorder: An overview of the literature*. London: Joint Working Party on Organisational Health and Welfare, Home Office.

Hillenberg, J. B. and Wolf, K. L. (1988) Psychological impact of traumatic events: Implications for employee assistance intervention. *Employee Assistance Quarterly*, **4**, 1–13.

Hockey, R. (Ed.) (1983) *Stress and Fatigue in Human Performance*. Chichester, UK: Wiley.

Hodgkinson, P. (1988) Psychological effects of transportation disaster. *Medicine Science and the Law*, **28**, 304–309.

Holdaway, S. (Ed.) (1979) *The British Police*. London: Edward Arnold.

Holdaway, S. (1980) Occupational culture of urban policing: An ethnographic study. Doctoral thesis, University of Sheffield.

Holdaway, S. (1989) Discovering structure: Studies of the British police occupational culture. In M. Weatheritt (Ed.), *Police Research: Some Future Prospects*. Aldershot, Avebury.

Holdaway, S. (1991) *Recruiting a Multiracial Police Force*. London, HMSO.

Home Office (1983) *Memorandum 114 on Efficiency, Economy and Effectiveness in the Police Service*. London: Home Office.

Home Office (1989) *Circular 87: Equal Opportunities: Policies in the Police Service*. London: Home Office.

Home Office (1990a) *Circular 33: Ethnic Minority Recruitment into the Police Service*. London: Home Office.

Home Office (1990b) *Hillsborough Stadium Disaster 15 April 1989: Inquiry. Final report*. London: Home Office.

Home Office (1991) *Circular 104: Career Development of Police Officers in England and Wales: Guidance to forces on good practice*. London: Home Office.

Home Office Science and Technology Group (1989) *A Review of*

Organisational Health and Welfare in the Police Service. London: PRSU, Home Office.

Horowitz, M. (1976) Diagnosis and treatment of stress response syndromes In H. J. Parad, H. L. P. Reswick and L. G. Parad (Eds), *Emergency and Disaster Management.* Bourie, MD: Charles Press.

House of Commons Home Affairs Committee (1991) *Police sickness.* London: HMSO.

Hunt, L. (1991) When I came out. *Police Review*, 19 April, 804–805.

Hurrel, J. (1977) *Job stress amongst police officers: A preliminary analysis.* US Dept of Health Education and Welfare (NIOSH). Washington, DC: US Government Printing Office.

Hyder, K. (1991) PLUS: below par. *Police Review*, 15 February, 322–323.

Inwald, R. E. (1984) Pre-employment psychological testing for law enforcement: Ethical and procedural issues. Washington Crime news service. *Training Aids Digest*, **9**, 1–6.

Jacobs, P. (1987) Women in policework: What's the attraction? *Free Inquiry in Creative Sociology*, **15**, 213–217.

Jacobs, P. (1988) Stress among female police officers: The times are they a changing. Paper presented to the meeting of the Academy of Criminal Justice Sciences in San Francisco, California.

Janis, I. (1972) *Victims of Groupthink.* Boston: Houghton Mifflin.

Jermier, J. M., Gaines, J. and McIntosh, N. J. (1989) Reactions to physically dangerous work: A conceptual and empirical analysis. *Journal of Organizational Behaviour*, **10**, 15–33.

Joint Working Party on Organisational Health and Welfare (1987) Counselling for police officers: Preliminary Guidelines. Unpublished report. London: Home Office.

Jones, D. R. (1985) Secondary disaster victims: The emotional effects of recovering and identifying human remains. *American Journal of Psychiatry*, **142**, 303–307.

Jones, J. C. and Barlow, D. H. (1990) The etiology of post traumatic stress disorder. *Clinical Psychology Review*, **10**, 299–328.

Jones, S. (1983) Community policing in Devon and Cornwall: Some research findings of the relationship between the public and the police. In T. Bennett (Ed.), *The Future of Police: Papers presented to the 15th Cropwood Round Table Conference.* Cambridge Institute of Criminology.

Jones, S. (1986) *Policewomen and Equality.* London: Macmillan.

Jones, S. (1987a) Making it work: Some reflections on the Sex Discrimination Act. *Police Journal*, **60**, 294–302.

Jones, S. (1987b) Policewomen: Caught in the act. *Policing*, **2**, 129–140.

Joyce, K. (1991) Women in policing: An analysis of senior officers' views. MA Dissertation, University of Surrey.

Kanter, R. M. (1977) Some effects of proportions on group life: Skewed sex ratios and responses to token women. *American Journal of Sociology*, **82**, 965–990.

Karasek, P., Baker, D., Marxer, F., Ahlbom, A. and Theorell, T. (1981) Job decision latitude, job demands and cardiovascular disease: A prospective study of Swedish men. *American Journal of Public Health*, **71**, 694–705.

Kasl, S. V. (1973) Mental health and work environment: An examination of the evidence. *Journal of Occupational Medicine*, **15**, (6), 509–517.

Kasl, S. V. and Cooper, C. L. (Eds) (1987) *Stress and Health: Issues in Research Methodology*. Chichester, UK: Wiley.

Kinsey, R. (1990) *Victimisation of the Silent Minorities*. University of Edinburgh Centre for Criminology.

Kirmeyer, S. and Diamond, A. (1985) Coping by police officers: A study of role stress and type A and type B behaviour patterns. *Journal of Occupational Behaviour*, **6**, 183–195.

Kirsta, A. K. (1988) *Victims Surviving the Aftermath of Violent Crime*. London: Century Hutchinson.

Kissman, K. (1990) Women in blue-collar occupations: An exploration of constraints and facilitators. *Journal of Sociology and Social Welfare*, **17**, 139–149.

Kolb, L. C. (1986) Treatment of chronic post-traumatic stress disorders. *Current Psychiatric Therapies*, **23**, 119–127.

Kroes, W. (1976) *Society's Victim, the Policeman: An Analysis of Job Stress in Policing*. New York: Charles C. Thomas.

Kroes, W. H. (1982) Job stress in policewomen: An empirical study. *Police Stress*, Winter, 10–11.

Kroes, W., Margolis, B., and Hurrel, J. (1974) Job stress in policemen. *Journal of Police Science and Administration*, **2**, 145–185.

Kuch, K., Swinson, R. and Kirby, M. (1985) Post-traumatic stress disorder after car accidents. *Canadian Journal of Psychiatry*, **30**, 426–427.

Leavitt, H. J. (1951) Some effects of certain communication patterns on group performance. *Journal of Abnormal and Social Psychology*, **46**, 38–50.

Lefkowitz, J. (1975) Psychological attributes of policemen: A review of research and opinion. *Journal of Social Issues*, **31**, 3–26.

Lewis, R. W. (1973) Towards an understanding of police anomie. *Journal of Police Science and Administration*, **1**, 484–490.

Lindgren, H. C. and Harvey, J. H. (1981) *An Introduction to Social Psychology* (3rd edn). St Louis: C. V. Mosby Company.

Loo, R. (1985) Police development for psychological services in the Royal Canadian Mounted Police. *Journal of Police Science and Administration*, **13**, 132–137.

Loo, R. (1986) Post-shooting stress reactions among police officers. *Journal of Human Stress*, **12**, 27–31.

Loo, R. (1987) Policies and programs for mental health in law enforcement organisations. *Canada's Mental Health* (September), 18–22.

Lowe, G. S. and Northcott, H. C. (1988) The impact of working conditions, social roles and personal characteristics on gender differences in disasters. *Work and Occupations*, **15**, 55–77.

Lunneborg, P. W. (1989) *Women Police Officers: Current Career Profile*. Springfield, Ill.: Charles C. Thomas.

McCammon, S., Durham, T. W., Allison, E. J. and Williamson, J. E. (1988) Emergency workers' cognitive appraisal and coping with traumatic events. *Journal of Traumatic Stress*, **1**, 352–372.

McDonald, I. (1989) With a little help from our friends. *Police Review*, 31 March, 653.

McFarlane, A. C. (1989) The aetiology of post-traumatic morbidity: Predisposing, precipitating and perpetuating factors. *British Journal of Psychiatry*, **154**, 221–228.

McFarlane, A. C. (1990) Vulnerability to Post-traumatic Stress Disorder. In M. E. Wolf and A. D. Mosnaim (Eds), *Post-traumatic Stress Disorder: Aetiology, Phenomenology and Treatment*. Washington, DC: American Psychiatric Press.

Malloy, T. E. and Mays, G. L. (1984) The police stress hypothesis: A critical evaluation. *Criminal Justice and Behaviour*, **11**, 197–224.

Malovich, N. and Stake, J. E. (1990) Sexual harassment on campus: Individual differences in attitudes and beliefs. *Psychology of Women Quarterly*, **14**, 63–81.

Malt, U. (1988) The long term psychiatric consequences of accident injury: A longitudinal study of 107 adults. *British Journal of Psychiatry*, **153**, 810–818.

Mann, J. P. and Neece, J. (1990) Workers' compensation for law enforcement related post traumatic stress disorder. *Behavioural Sciences and the Law*, **8**, 447–456.

Manning, P. K. (1978) The social control of police work. In S. Holdaway (Ed.), *The British Police*. London: Edward Arnold.

Manning, P. K. (1991) Technological dramas and the police: Statement and counterstatement in organisational analysis. Paper presented to Seminar Series on Executive Issues, July 17–19. Texas: Law Enforcement Management Institute.

Manolias, M. (1983) A preliminary study of stress in the police service. London: Home Office, SRDB, Human Factors Group.

Manolias, M. and Hyatt-Williams, A. (1986) Post-shooting experiences in firearms officers. London: Joint Working Party on Organisational Health and Welfare, Home Office.

March, J. S. (1990) The nosology of post-traumatic stress disorder. *Journal of Anxiety Disorders*, **4**, 61–82.

Margolis, B. L. (1973) Stress is a work hazard too. *Industrial Medicine Occupational Health and Surgery*, **42**, 20–23.

Marmot, M. and Madge, N. (1987) An epidemiological perspective on stress and health. In S. V. Kasl and C. L. Cooper (Eds), *Stress and Health: Issues in Research Methodology*. Chichester, UK: Wiley.

Martelli, T. A, Waters, L. C. and Martelli, J. (1989) The police stress survey: Reliability in relation to job satisfaction and organisational commitment. *Psychological Reports*, **64**, 267–273.

Martin, C. A., McKean, H. E. and Veltkamp, L. J. (1986) Post-traumatic stress disorder in police and working with victims: A pilot study. *Journal of Police Science and Administration*, **14**, 98–101.

Martin, P. W. (1990) A survey to establish effects of traumatic incidents on police officers and how those officers seek help, to include officers' attitudes to the use of Counselling Schemes. Unpublished dissertation, Department of Sociology, University of Surrey, UK.

Martin, S. E. (1979) Policewomen and policewomen: Occupational role dilemmas and choices of female officers. *Journal of Police Science and Administration*, **7**, 314–323.

Martin, S. E. (1980) *Breaking and Entering*. Berkeley, Cal.: University of California Press.

Martin, S. E. (1989) Women in policing: The eighties and beyond. In Kenney, D. J. (Ed.), *Police and Policing; Contemporary Issues*. New York: Praeger, pp. 3–16.

Marwick, A. (1977) *Women at War* 1914–1918. London: Fontana.

Mason, G. (1988) Are civilians second class policemen? *Police Review*, 1 July, 1374–1375.

Maypole D. E. and Skaine, R. (1982) Sexual harassment of blue collar workers. *Journal of Sociology and Social Welfare*, **9**, 682–695.

Meager M. S. and Yentes N. A. (1986) Choosing a career in policing: A comparison of male and female perceptions. *Journal of Police Science and Administration*, **14**, 320–327.

Megranahan, M. (1989) Counselling in the workplace. In W. Dryden, D. Charles-Edwards and R. Woolfe (Eds), *Handbook of Counselling in Britain*. London: Tavistock/Routledge.

Melancon, D. (1985) Quality circles: The shape of things to come. In J. J. Pyfe (Ed.), *Police Management Today: Issues and Case Studies*. Washington, DC: ICMA.

Mendelson, G. (1987) Concept of post-traumatic stress-disorder: A review. *International Journal of Law and Psychiatry*, **10**, 45–62.

Mezey, G. and Rubenstein, H. (1992) Sexual harassment: The problem and its consequences. *Journal of Forensic Psychiatry*, **3**, 221–233.

Milham, S. (1983) *Occupational Mortality in Washington State 1950–59*. DHHS (NIOSH) Publication No. 83-116. Washington, DC: US Government Printing Office.

Miller, I. (1992) Stress inoculation training for police D.V.I. teams: A practical approach. Paper presented to the World Conference of the International Society for Traumatic Stress Studies, Amsterdam, The Netherlands. June 1992.

Mirrlees-Black, C. (1992) *Using psychometric personality tests in the selection of fire arms officers*. Home Office Research and Planning Unit Paper 68. London: HMSO.

Mitchell, E. (1991) Perceived stress in frontline officers. Birmingham, UK: Unpublished report to the West Midlands Police Force.

Mitchell, J. and Bray, B. (1990) *Emergency Services Stress: Guidelines for Preserving the Health and Careers of Emergency Services Personnel*. Englewood Cliffs, NJ: Prentice-Hall.

Mitchell, J. T. (1983) When disaster strikes ... the critical incident stress debriefing process. *Journal of Emergency and Medical Services*, **8**, 36–39.

Monk, T. H. (1988) Coping with the stress of shift work. *Work and Stress*, **2**, 169–172.

Moriarty, A. and Field, M. W. (1990) Proactive intervention: A new approach to police EAP programs. *Public Personnel Management*, **19**, 155–161.

Murphy, L. R. (1984) Occupational stress management: A review and appraisal. *Journal of Occupational Psychology*, **57**, 1–15.

Myers, D. G. (1989) Mental health and disaster: Preventive approaches to intervention. In R. Gist and B. Lubin (Eds), *Psychosocial Aspects of Disaster*. Chichester, UK: Wiley.

National Welfare Officers' Conference (1987) Report to the Association of Chief Police Officers. Unpublished report. London.

Neidig, P. H., Russell, H. E. and Seng, A. F. (1992) Interspousal aggression in law enforcement families: A preliminary investigation. *Police Studies*, **15**, 30–38.

Neyroud, P. (1992) *Multi-agency approach to racial harassment*. London: Police Requirements Support Unit, Home Office.

Norris, R., Carroll, D. and Cochrane, R. (1990) The effects of aerobic and anaerobic training on fitness, blood pressure and psychological stress and well being. *Journal of Psychosomatic Research*, **34**, 367–375.

Office of Population Census and Surveys (1988) *Occupational Mortality*. Series DS No. 6. London: HMSO.

Office of Population Census and Surveys (1989) *General Household Survey 20*. London: Social Surveys Division, OPCS.

O'Leary, J. (1981) Homosexuals in the police. In G. Henderson (Ed.), *Police Human Relations*. Springfield, Ill: Charles C. Thomas.

O'Neill, S. (1990) Are the police looking the other way? *The Independent*, Tuesday 18 December.

Operational Policing Review (1990) London: Association of Chief Police Officers.

Ott, E. M. (1989) Effects of the male–female ratio at work: Policewomen and male nurses. *Psychology of Women Quarterly*, **13**, 41–57.

Payne, R. (1991) Taking stock of corporate culture. *Personnel Management*, July, 26–29.

Pendergrass, V. E. and Ostrove, N. M. (1984) A survey of stress in women in policing. *Journal of Police Science and Administration*, **12**, 303–309.

Phillips, S. and Cochrane, R. (1991) *Assaults Against the Police: A Study in Three Stages. Final report*. Birmingham, UK: University of Birmingham.

Picquet, D. C. and Best, R. A. (1986) *Post-traumatic Stress Disorder, Rape Trauma, Delayed Stress and Related Conditions: A Bibliography*. Jefferson, Mo.: McFarland & Co.

Plant, M. A. (1981) Risk factors in employment. In B. D. Hore and M. A. Plant (Eds), *Alcohol Problems in Employment*. London: Croom Helm.

Pogrebin, M. (1986) The changing role of women: Female police officers' occupational problems. *Police Journal*, **59**, 127–133.

Poole, E. D. and Pogrebin, M. R. (1988) Factors affecting the decision to remain in the police: A study of women officers. *Journal of Police Science and Administration*, **16**, 49–55.

Pope, K. E. and Pope, D. W. (1986) Attitudes of male police officers towards their female counterparts. *Police Journal*, **59**, 242–250.

Poyner, B. and Warne, C. (1986) *Violence to Staff: A Basis for Assessment and Prevention*. London: HMSO.

Powell, G., Edelmann, R. J., Campbell, E. A. and Thrush, D. (1992) A report on the functioning of Surrey's Constabulary Force Counselling Service: The first hundred clients. Department of Psychology, University of Surrey, UK.

Price, B. R. (1974) A study of leadership strength of female police executives. *Journal of Police Science and Administration*, **2**, 219–226.

Punch, M. (1979) The secret social service. In S. Holdaway (Ed.), *The British Police*. London: Edward Arnold.

Radford, J. (1989) Women and policing: Contradictions old and new. In J. Hanmer, J. Radford and E. Stanko (Eds), *Women Policing and Male Violence*. London: Routledge.

Raphael, B. (1986) *When Disaster Strikes: A Handbook for the Caring Professions*. London: Unwin Hyman.

Raphael, B., Singh, B., Bradbury, L. et al (1983–84) Who helps the helpers? The effects of a disaster on the rescue workers. *Omega*, **14**, 9–20.

Reese, J. T. and Goldstein, H. A. (1986) *Psychological Services for Law Enforcement*. Washington, DC: US Government Printing Office.

Reichman, W. and Beidel, B. E. (1989) Implementation of a state police EAP. *Journal of Drug Issues*, **19**, 369–383.

Reilly, B. J. and DiAngelo, J. A. (1990) Communication: A cultural system of meaning and value. *Human Relations*, **43**, 129–140.

Reiner, R. (1979) Police unionism. In S. Holdaway (Ed.), *The British Police*. London: Edward Arnold.

Reiner, R. (1985) *The Politics of the Police*. New York: Harvester Wheatsheaf.

Reiner, R. (1991) *Chief Constables: Bobbies, Bosses or Bureaucrats*. Oxford: Oxford University Press.

Reiser, M. (1974) Some organisational stresses on policemen. *Journal of Police Science and Administration*, **2**, 156–159.

Reiser, M. (1976) Stress, distress and adaptation in police work. *The Police Chief*, January, 14–27.

Reiser, M. (1982) *Police Psychology*. California: Lehu Publishing.

Richards, J. (1987) Appraisal sex scandal. *Times Higher Educational Supplement*, 18 December, 12.

Richman, J. (1983) *Traffic Wardens: An Ethnography of Street Administration*. Manchester, UK: Manchester University Press.

Robinson, P. (1981) Stress in the police service. *Police Review*, November, 2254–2259, 2308–2312; December, 2364–2367, 2412–2414.

Rodie, J. and McGurk, B. (1989) Keeping an open mind about psychology. *Police Review*, 7 April, 713.

Rosa, R. R, Colligan, M. J. and Lewis, P. (1989) Extended workdays: Effects of 8 hour and 12 hour rotating shift schedules on performance, subjective alertness, sleep patterns and psychosocial variables. *Work and Stress*, **3**, 21–32.

Rose, D. (1990) Forces of change. *Guardian*, 21 February.

Rosenhan, D. L. and Seligman, M. E. P. (1984) *Abnormal Psychology*. New York: W. W. Norton.

Royal Ulster Constabulary (1992) *Chief Constable's Annual Report*. Belfast: Royal Ulster Constabulary.

Rubenstein, M. (1988) *The dignity of women at work: A report on the problem of sexual harassment in the member States of the European Communities* (PO As 1 1-11). Luxemburg: Office for Official Publications of the EC.

Ruch, L. O., Chandler, S. M. and Harter, R. A. (1980) Life change and rape impact. *Journal of Health and Social Behaviour*, **21**, 248–260.

Ruddock, R. (1974) Recruit training stress vs non stress. *Police Chief*, November, 47–50.

Sadu, G., Cooper, C. and Allison, T. (1989) A Post Office initiative to stamp out stress. *Personnel Management*, August, 40–44.

Sandler, G. B. and Mintz, E. (1974) Police organisations, their changing internal and external relationships. *Journal of Police Science and Administration*, **1**, 458–463.

Scurfield, R. M. (1985) Post-trauma stress assessment and treatment: Overview and formulations. In C. R. Figley (Ed.), *Trauma and its Wake*. New York: Brunner/Mazel.

Selye, H. (1956) *The Stress of Life*. New York: McGraw-Hill.

Sewell, J.D. (1986) Administrative concerns in law enforcement stress management. *Police Studies*, **9**, 153–159.

Sewell, J. D. and Crew, L. (1984) The forgotten victim, stress and the police dispatcher. *FBI Law Enforcement Bulletin*, March, 7–11.

Sharrock, D. (1988) Police set up unit for stress crisis. *Guardian*, 28 October.

Shaw, B. (1989) Quality circles and the British police. *Police Journal*, **LXII**, 87–104.

Sheerman, B. (1991) What Labour wants. *Policing*, **7**, Autumn, 194–203.

Sherman, L. (1975) An evaluation of policewomen on patrol in a suburban police department. *Journal of Police Science and Administration*, **5**, 434–438.

Shepherd, M. and Hodgkinson, P. E. (1990) The hidden victims of disaster: Helper stress. *Stress Medicine*, **6**, 29–35.

Silvester, G. (1989) Reasons for the premature voluntary resignation of graduates from the police service. Manchester, UK: Greater Manchester Police.

Smith, D. J. (1983) *Police and People in London III: A Survey of Police Officers*. London: Policy Studies Institute Report 620.

Smith, D. J. and Gray, J. (1985) *Police and the People of London: The PSI Report*. Aldershot: Gower.

Smith, M. and Gibson, J. (1988) Using repertory grids to investigate racial prejudice. *Applied Psychology*, **37**, 4, 311–326.

Sokoloff, N. J., Raffel-Price, B. and Kuleshnyk, I. (1992) A case study of black and white women police in an urban police department. *Justice Professional*, **6**, 68–85.

Somodevilla, S. A. (1978) The psychologist's role in the Police Department. *Police Chief*, **39**, 21–23.

Souryal, S. S. (1981) *Police Organisation and Administration*. New York: Harcourt Brace Jovanovich.

Steel, B. S. and Lovrich, N. P. (1987) Equality and efficiency trade offices, in affirmative action, real or imagined? The case of women in policing. *Social Science Journal*, **24**, 53–70.

Stockdale, J. (1991) Sexual harassment at work. In J. Firth Cozens and M. West (Eds), *Women at Work: Psychological and Organisation Perspectives*. Milton Keynes, UK: Open University Press.

Stratton, J. (1980) Psychological services for police. *Journal of Police Science and Administration*, **3**, 31–39.

Stratton, J. G, Parker, D. A. and Shibbe, J. R. (1984) Post-traumatic stress: Study of police officers involved in shootings. *Psychological Reports*, **55**, 127–131.

Symonds, M. (1970) Emotional hazards of police work. *American Journal of Psychoanalysis*, **30**, 155–160.

Tafoya, W. I. (1986) A Delphi forecast of the future of law enforcement. Doctoral dissertation, University of Maryland.

Territo, L. and Vetter, H. J. (1981) *Stress and Police Personnel*. Boston, MA: Allyn & Bacon.

Terry, W. C. (1981) Police stress: The empirical evidence. *Journal of Police Science and Administration*, **9**, 61–75.

Toch, H. (1973) Psychological consequences of the police role. In Eldefonso (Ed.), *Readings in Criminal Justice*. New York: Glencoe Press.

Touche Ross (1992) *Consultancy study into effective shift systems for the police service*. London: Touche Ross.

Uniform Crime Reports (1988) *Law enforcement officers killed in the line of duty*. Washington, DC: US Department of Justice.

Van Mannen, J. and Schein, E. H. (1979) Towards a theory of organisational socialisation. In B. M. Shaw (Ed.), *Research into Organisational Behaviour*, Vol. 1, pp. 209–264.

Vega, M. and Silverman, I. (1982) Female police officers as viewed by their male counterparts. *Police Studies*, **5**, 31–39.

Violanti, J. M., Marshall, J. R. and Howe, B. (1983) Police occupational demands, psychological distress and the coping function of alcohol. *Journal of Occupational Medicine*, **25**, (6), 455–458.

Violanti, J. M., Vena, J. E. and Marshall, J. R. (1986) Disease risk and mortality among police officers: New evidence and contributing factors. *Journal of Police Science and Administration*, **14**, 17–23.

Wagner, H. (1986) Belastungen in Polizei beruf. Ammerkungen zu Diagnosie und Therapie. *Munchen Polizei*, **77**, 80–84.

Wagoner, C. P. (1976) Police alienation: Some sources and implications.

Journal of Police Science and Administration, 4, 389–403.

Walklate, S. (1992) Jack and Jill join up at Sun Hill: Public images of police officers. *Policing and Society,* 2, 219–232.

Wareing, R. and Morgan, R. (1988) Need for re-assessment. *Police Review,* 13 May.

Weatheritt, M. (1986) *Innovations in Policing.* Beckenham, UK: Croom Helm.

Webb, S. D. and Smith, D. L. (1980) Police stress: A conceptual overview. *Journal of Criminal Justice,* 8, 251–257.

Wexler, J. G. and Logan, D. D. (1983) Sources of stress among women police officers. *Journal of Police Science and Administration,* 11, 46–53.

White, S. (1982) Police suicide: What are the causes? An investigative report with particular reference to the Royal Ulster Constabulary. Unpublished report. Bramshill Police Staff College, UK.

Wilke, H. and Van Knippenberg, A. (1988) in M. Hewstone, W. Stroebe, J.-P. Codol and G. M. Stephenson (Eds), *Introduction to Social Psychology: A European Perspective.* Oxford: Blackwell.

Wilkinson, C. B. and Vera, E. (1989). Clinical responses to disaster: Assessment, management and treatment. In R. Gist and B. Lubin (Eds), *Psychosocial Aspects of Disaster.* New York: Wiley.

Wilson, J. Q. (1968) *City Politics and Public Policy.* New York: Wiley.

Wilson, P. (1987) The police and the future: Social trends and their implications for law enforcement. *Australian Police Journal,* 41, 99–104.

Wilson, R. R. and Western, J. S. (1972) *The Policeman's Position Today and Tomorrow: An Examination of the Victoria Police Force.* St Lucia: University of Queensland Press.

Witherspoon, S. (1989). Interim report: A woman's work. In R. Jowell, S. Witherspoon and L. Brook (Eds), *British Social Attitudes: The 5th Report.* London: Social Community Planning Research, pp. 175–194.

Wolff Olins (1988) A force for change: A report on the corporate identity of the Metropolitan police. London: Wolff Olins

Woolfenden, S. (1989). Police absenteeism: Its meaning, measurement and control. Paper presented to the Home Office Police Requirement Support Unit Conference, Exeter, 25–26 October.

Woolfenden, S. (1991) Sickness wastage, causes and solutions. Paper presented to Quality through Equality Conference. Bramshill Police Training College, 23–26 March.

Young, M. A. (1984) Police wives. In H. Callan and S. Ardener (Eds), *Incorporated Wives.* London: Croom Helm.

Young, M. A. (1989) Crime, violence and terrorism. In R. Gist and B. Lubin (Eds), *Psychosocial Aspects of Disaster.* New York: Wiley.

Young, M. A. (1991) *An Inside Job.* Oxford: Clarendon Press.

Index

Index compiled by Jenny Ward